3.25

DAT

The Theatre

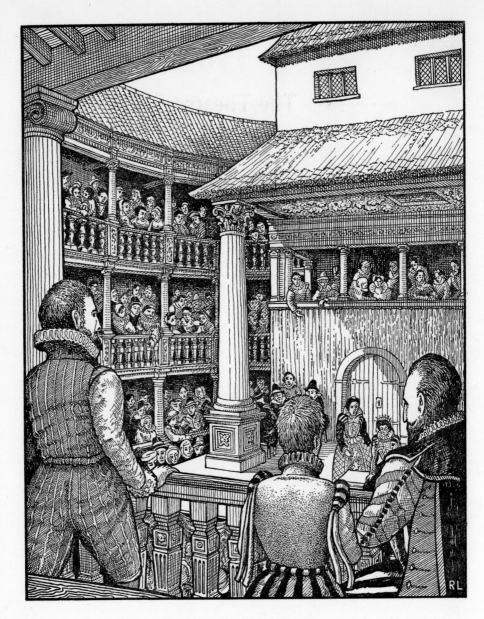

A theatre in Shakespeare's time

THE THEATRE

by Helen & Richard Leacroft

Illustrated by Richard Leacroft
together with some drawings from original sources

ROY PUBLISHERS NEW YORK

First published 1958
Reprinted 1961

TO

THE THEATRE ROYAL

LEICESTER

1836–1958

in grateful memory

PRINTED IN GREAT BRITAIN

Contents

Acknowledgements

The authors would like to thank all those who have helped with criticism or advice in the preparation of this book, with particular thanks to Mr. Sydney Reed. They would also like to acknowledge their debt to all those authors whose works on the Theatre have formed the background to their theatrical lives, and must therefore have influenced their thoughts on the subject.

Thanks are also due to the Edinburgh Festival Society and the Questor's Theatre for supplying information on which to base the drawings of their stages, to the 'Architectural Review' for permission to quote the extract on page 58, to Benjamin Pollock, Ltd., for permission to reproduce the pictures on pages 53–55, and to the 'Journal of the Royal Institute of British Architects' for the use of the block on page 50.

Buffalo dance of the Okippe Indians
(after an original painting, by permission of the University of California)

THE house lights are lowered, the foot-lights illumine the golden fringe and tassels of the red velvet curtain. A hush falls over the audience and suddenly, away goes the curtain and through the picture-frame a new world is revealed: perhaps a brightly-lit Christmas Panto-mime is displayed before us, or the blasted heath where Macbeth meets the three weird sisters, or we may look into an ordinary room from which one wall has been removed, and watch the happenings in the lives of the people who live there.

This is the picture that most of us see in our mind's eye when we think about the theatre, whether the per-formance takes place in a proper theatre or in a community or school hall which has been transformed from its work-a-day look by the magic of Theatre.

But the Theatre has not always been shut up in an imposing building, with special seats for the audience who see the actor performing behind an opening in one wall of the auditorium. The stage has not always been so elaborately equipped with scenery and machinery, at times it has been no more than a few planks laid across trestles to raise the players above their thronging audience.

As the art of the dramatist, the actor and the scenic artist grew, so the stage and the theatre developed to meet their needs. In this book we shall show you how the theatre has slowly altered and been adapted, sometimes for good, sometimes for bad, until it became our present-day picture-frame theatre.

I

Egyptian funeral. The priest on the right is dressed as the god Anubis

EARLY DRAMA

The early dramatic attempts of all peoples were much the same; the first expression to emerge being dancing, a natural form of joy or excitement. The most developed emotion of primitive peoples was one of religion and Man's desire to propitiate the gods to ensure a good harvest, a plentiful supply of rain or the fertility of his flocks and herds took the form of communal religious dances led by the priests or witch doctors.

One of the earliest dramas comes from Ancient Egypt; it is part of a dramatic funeral rite to ensure the safe passage through the underworld of the dead Pharaoh, and was performed by priests dressed in animal-headed masks to represent gods. The only 'play' that has survived from those early times is the Osiris Passion, sometimes called the Abydos Passion, taking this name from the place where it was performed. This play deals in dramatic form with the killing of the god, Osiris, the cutting up and hiding in various places of his body, and the efforts of Isis, his sister-wife, and his son Horus to find the pieces and put the body together again so that it might be used as the home of the god's spirit or *ka*. It was performed in front of a temple and the audience took part in the various fights which occurred. As yet there was no need for a special theatre building, the plays having a religious content could well be performed in, or before, the temple.

ANCIENT GREECE

The Ancient Greeks believed in nature spirits and they performed dances to them for which they disguised themselves in goat skins and tails. One of the most important of the Greek gods was Dionysius, the god of the vine, and the dances were soon transferred to his honour. As Greece is a very mountainous country the only levelled areas in many villages would have been the circular threshing floors, and it was here that the dionysiac dances, in which the whole village took part, were probably first performed. By the 6th century, B.C., these dances, which were of a religious nature, took place each year at two great festivals; the first in the spring, signifying the re-awakening of the earth, and the second in the autumn at the completion of the harvest. Offerings to the god were taken in procession to the altar and the sacrifice of a goat was accompanied by songs and dances. During the spring festival a hymn called the Dithyramb was sung; this incorporated a song and dance performed by a group, or chorus, accompanied by a flute-player, and incidents from the life of the god were mimed. This was the last development in which the community as a whole performed.

As the performance became traditional and familiar, interest centred on the way in which the performers made the spirits behave, and so they had to make their characterizations more realistic; to do this speech was needed and this was added to the dithyramb when it came under the control of Arion of Lesbos. He divided a chorus of fifty into two groups and inserted verses which were spoken by a leader, thus creating a simple dialogue. It was from these goat songs and dances that the great tragedies of the Greek theatre developed. The word tragedy came from the Greek word *tragos*, which was the name given to the goat sacrificed at the festival. It remained for Thespis of Ikaria (early 6th century), a Greek poet, to introduce the first actor as distinct from the chorus leader. This actor delivered spoken verse at the same time imitating the person with whom the story dealt. Thespis, wearing an unpainted linen mask, performed this task standing on the sacrificial table near the altar so that he might be seen above the heads of the chorus.

Tradition says that Thespis took his band of players around the countryside on a cart which they set up and used as a platform. Performances could therefore have taken place on any suitable site; in the towns this was probably the market place or *agora*. Many early market places had arrangements of steps where important persons might stand or sit to watch a performance: examples can be seen in some of the ruined towns of Ancient Crete. It soon became necessary to provide a special place where theatrical performances could be held, and one of the earliest examples of these 'theatres' can be seen at Ikaria, where Thespis was born. This adjoined the agora and consisted of an earth slope on which the audience sat, separated by a row of dedicatory tablets—*stelai*—and a row of seats of honour—*prohedria*—from a rectangular dancing floor or *orchestra*, bounded on its far side by a terrace wall. In later theatres there were timber benches for the audience, but eventually these were replaced by stone.

Early Greek theatre at Ikaria, 5th or 4th century B.C.

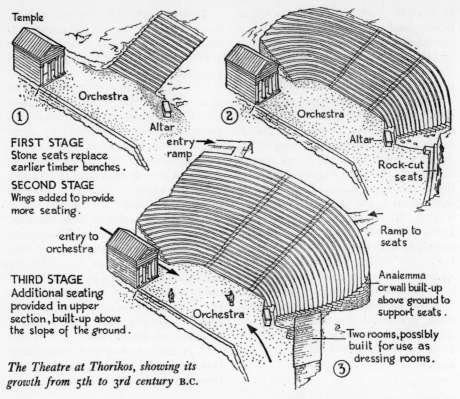

Temple

Orchestra

① **FIRST STAGE**
Stone seats replace
earlier timber benches.

SECOND STAGE
Wings added to provide
more seating.

Altar

② Orchestra

Altar

entry
ramp

Rock-cut
seats

entry to
orchestra

THIRD STAGE
Additional seating
provided in upper
section, built-up above
the slope of the ground.

Orchestra

Ramp to
seats

Analemma
or wall built-up
above ground to
support seats.

Two rooms, possibly
built for use as
dressing rooms.

③

*The Theatre at Thorikos, showing its
growth from 5th to 3rd century* B.C.

On the site of the sea port of Thorikos are the remains of such a proper theatre, and it is possible to see how the shape of this theatre changed to accommodate more people. The earliest portion of the auditorium or *cavea*, consisted of a rect-angular block of straight stone seats; to this two curved wings were added and later a rear section. We are reminded of the religious nature of these performances by the presence of a small temple. We cannot be certain if the performances held on the circular threshing floors influenced the shape of later theatres, or if these evolved along the lines we have

just seen; but, whichever the case, the theatre that came into being, and which we think of as a typical Greek theatre had a circular orchestra with stone seating arranged around it in a horse-shoe to slightly more than a semi-circle on the slope of an existing hillside.

About thirty years after the introduc-tion of the actor, Greek drama in Athens began to assume the form with which we are familiar. The drama was still a reli-gious observance and the audience, con-sisting of the whole population of the state was participating in an act of wor-ship. The Dionysiac Festivals started

4

Greek comedy masks

very early in the morning and continued for three days throughout the hours of daylight. Three poets were chosen and each given one day on which to perform his works, which consisted of three tragedies, a satyr-play and an interlude; at the conclusion of the festival the poet judged to have been most successful was crowned with an ivy wreath, a sign of great honour.

The tragedies were based on myths, already familiar to the audience, and dealt with the inevitable fate of a central character, either king or noble man, which was brought about by the interference of the gods in the affairs of mortals. In the satyr-play the main character of the tragedy was often introduced with a company of satyrs, half animal, half human creatures and the rough action consisted of wild jests and dances.

The theatre was a state institution, the dramatist had to apply to the magistrates for permission to have his plays performed. If the plays were considered to be of a sufficiently high standard the poet was given his chief actor—*protagonist*—and, as the plays became more elaborate, a *choregus*. The choregus was a rich citizen chosen by the magistrates to bear the cost of the production; this was looked upon as a great honour and was a tax willingly borne. The choregus chose and paid the chorus: he also provided a trainer to teach them their movements and speech and supervise their health, and he hired a flute-player and any crowd performers who might be needed.

It was the poet Aeschylus (525–456 B.C.) who introduced the second actor into the plays and the third was first used by Sophocles (495–405 B.C.). Thus when the theatre of Greece was at its height three actors were required, who portrayed all the characters, including the female ones. They played several roles by changing masks; for example in the 'Hippolytus', by Euripides (484–406 B.C.), the protagonist probably played both the king and Phaedra in addition to other smaller roles.

It was not until 486 B.C. that comedies were performed at the festivals. The first form, *Old Comedy* consisted of plays in which the people and the state were ridiculed and the plots were usually fantastic. The *New Comedy*, the greatest exponent of which was Menander (342–292 B.C.), was a comedy of manners using stock characters and dealing with domestic affairs. The comic actors wore masks and grotesque padding.

Masks were made of linen stretched over wood; they had large open-mouth pieces which may have served as a form of megaphone, increasing the resonance of the voice and ensuring that it could be heard all over the large cavea. The masks were so designed that the audience could instantly recognise a character, and the forehead—*onkos*—was elongated with a stylised hair arrangement, the hair being coloured to suit the part—grey or white

5

Greek comic actor

Greek tragic actor

Dancing slave

for an elderly person, dark hair for a young man, while slaves were given red hair. Each mask portrayed the predominant emotion and had to be changed when happiness turned to grief. In addition to the stylised masks the colour and type of garments were also conventional: a king or queen wore purple robes, a shepherd a short leather tunic; long trailing robes expressed grief and a character in exile was dressed in robes of grey or dirty white; the wearing of a hat signified that the character was undertaking a journey. Underneath his robe—*chiton*—the actor wore padding; he also wore boots with very thick soles called *kothornus*, these, together with the onkos, increased his height by at least a foot.

When the actors had to represent various characters it became necessary for them to have a changing room, and at the same time a place was needed to represent the palace or home of the protagonist. A hut or booth—*skene*—may first have been provided in the manner suggested at Thorikos (page 4), but at the Theatre of

Dionysius in Athens a skene, with a large central door, was erected and formed a backing to the orchestra. In successive rebuildings of the skene the central door was flanked by two lesser doors and further openings were added in the side wings—*paraskenia*—which projected to-

Figure of Greek tragic actor, in high mask and thick-soled boots (the lower projections are pegs for fixing the figure in a base)

6

Early Greek skene, with paraskenia

wards the audience. Temporary structures were sometimes built in front of the skene to represent various buildings, and the action of most plays was limited to the street or place in front of the houses of the characters; these were represented by the different doors.

Nobody really knows when a raised stage was first used. In early times both actors and chorus performed on the same level, but as the actors became more important than the chorus, a raised stage—*logeion*—was introduced. In the developed theatre this was some ten to twelve feet high and was supported at the front on a series of pillars, these are sometimes called the *proskenion* but this term is more generally applied to the whole stage structure in front of the skene. The actors entered the raised stage through the doors which were now raised to the higher level, and also by ramps which led up to the ends of the logeion. The chorus entered the orchestra through an entry way—*parodos*—in front of these ramps, and a typical Greek theatre may well have looked like the one shown here.

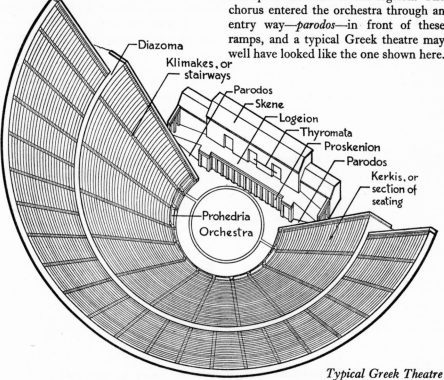

Typical Greek Theatre

7

In some later theatres, particularly those of Asia Minor, the three doors in the skene were replaced by openings called *thyromata*. It is thought that these may have been curtained and used for the performance of interior scenes. As it would have been difficult for the audience sitting in the semi-circular cavea to see into these openings, it may well have been the custom that when a particular curtain was open the area of stage in front was accepted as being part of the room behind the curtain; the actors could then come forward and play the scene whilst the audience, accepting the convention, thought of them as being inside the room.

Many scenic devices were used; the *deus ex machina* is thought to have been a crane operated from the roof of the stage building which enabled actors to be lowered from, or lifted up to, heaven. Scenes which took place off-stage were set up as tableaux and wheeled before the audience on platforms—*eccyclema*—; this device was used to show scenes of murder or violence which were not allowed to take place before the spectators. Thunder was made by dropping leaden balls on to tightly-stretched leather—*bronteion*.

Scenery in the form of painted panels—*pinakes*—was set between the pillars supporting the front of the stage and also in the thyromata. To show a change of scene further triangular units of scenery —*periaktoi*—were set behind some of the openings where they could be revolved.

In addition to these stone theatres there were also simple wooden stages which could easily be fitted up or taken down and carried around from place to place. These consisted of a raised stage with a curtained backing providing both a scenic background and a dressing room for the actors who performed comic plays of a broad and popular nature. It is interesting to note that this simple arrangement kept reappearing through the ages as you can see on pages 12 and 23.

Stage for a Greek comedy, after a vase painting

A Greek theatre

You may notice when you look at the drawings that the Greek theatre was not altogether successful as a place for performing the developed plays. When the theatres first developed their horse-shoe shape the attention of the audience was on a chorus performing songs and dances in the orchestra, but, as the drama became more realistic and each actor had something special to show or say, each member of the audience wished to see him clearly. This was not always possible when the stages were set up beyond the circular orchestra, so the Greeks began to cut off the seats at the end of the horseshoe and brought the stage nearer to the audience.

THE ROMAN THEATRE

When the Romans conquered Greece they altered many of the theatres, laying paving stones in the orchestras which the Greeks had kept as beaten earth or sand, and building new stages closer to the audience. Because they liked realistic shows they often enclosed the orchestra with a low wall to protect the audience when gladiatorial fights were in progress, or when wild animals were used, or even to allow the orchestra to be flooded so that a sea-fight might take place.

The Greeks built their theatres on the slopes of hills, but as the Romans often had to build their theatres on flat land they had to erect the seating on great vaults enclosed within a massive wall. They made the buildings as compact as possible by reducing the seating and orchestra to a semi-circle and by building the stage close to them. The entries to the orchestra were arched over with seats of honour above them and a colonnade—porticus—was built around the top of the auditorium. Although early Roman theatres were simple timber structures their later stone buildings were usually very ornate, being overdecorated with sculpture and rich marbles, especially the frons scenae, that is the rear wall of the stage forming the front wall of the scene room. Scenery is thought to have been used and the introduction of a curtain, dropping into a slot at the front of the stage, may have meant that scene changes could be made out of sight of the audience. The Roman stage was lower than the Greek and was connected to the orchestra by steps; when this was not needed for a production it was filled with seats for the audience.

In the Greek theatre only the important members of the audience had been protected from the sun by canopies over their seats, but the shape of the Roman theatre allowed for a great canvas covering—velarium—over the whole of the auditorium. Some smaller theatres were built within rectangular walls making it possible to cover the building with a timber roof providing permanent protection from the weather.

The actors were usually slaves, many having been brought from Greece; one such actor was Roscius, who achieved great fame and is said to have introduced the mask to the Roman theatre. Costumes were similar to those of the Greeks, and many of the plays were translations from the Greek tragedies, while the writers Terence and Plautus based much of their work on the comedies of Menander. The general feeling, however, was towards trivial, luxurious and decadent presentations and a popular form of theatre was that presented by the mimi. These mimi

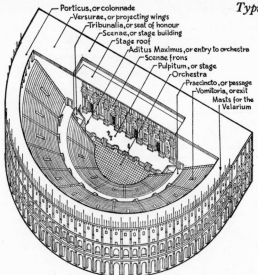

Porticus, or colonnade
Versurae, or projecting wings
Tribunalia, or seat of honour
Scenae, or stage building
Stage roof
Aditus Maximus, or entry to orchestra
Scenae frons
Pulpitum, or stage
Orchestra
Praecincto, or passage
Vomitoria, or exit
Masts for the Velarium

were troupes of players, including women, who travelled around and set up their wooden stages wherever they could gather an audience. Their entertainment was of a farcical nature and included singing, dancing and acrobatics. The characters which the mimi created may well have been the forerunners of the Commedia dell'Arte.

With the fall of the Roman Empire organised theatre in Western Europe fell into decay and finally disuse, even the more debased forms being infrequent. The Christian Church played a great part in this disintegration by its attacks on the plays and performers, decrees being passed forbidding baptism to anyone connected with the stage.

THE MIDDLE AGES

Throughout the dark ages only a primitive form of theatre was kept alive in Western Europe by small bands of performers, singers, minstrels and jongleurs. The new spring of drama was to flow from the Christian Church itself; as all services were sung in Latin the priests began to dramatise parts so that the congregation could understand the Christian story. The earliest example of these dramatic presentations is to be found in a *Concordia Regularis* written in the tenth century by Ethelwold, Bishop of Westminster.

On Good Friday a cross representing the body of Jesus was wrapped in cloths and placed in the Easter Sepulchre. On Easter Day a priest, dressed in an alb, entered and sat by the sepulchre. To him came three other priests, representing women, wearing copes and bearing in their hands thuribles of incense and walking as though seeking something. The first priest, representing the angel, then

Strolling players with platform stage

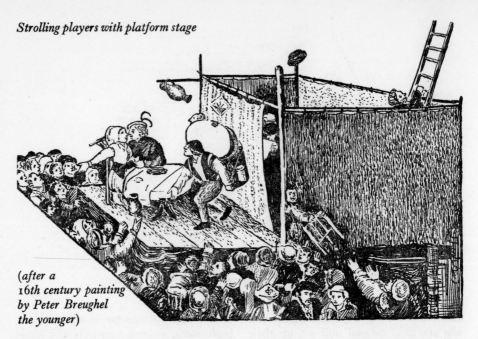

(after a
16th century painting
by Peter Breughel
the younger)

sang in Latin, "Whom seek ye in the sepulchre, O Christian women?" The three then replied, "Jesus of Nazareth, the crucified, O heavenly one." The angel answered, "He is not here, He is risen as He foretold. Go and announce that He is risen from the dead." The women turned to the congregation and sang, "Alleluia! The Lord is risen!" The angel lifting the veil from the sepulchre showed it empty save for the cloths in which the cross had been wrapped.

From these early beginnings further portions of the services were dramatised until simple plays evolved, these were performed inside the churches and in many they were eventually produced in a most realistic and spectacular manner. There are records that in Florence a performance was given on a scaffold erected in the nave, the congregation crowding round to marvel at the Throne of God surrounded by hundreds of lights and children dressed as angels playing music on cymbals, flutes and harps. A special contrivance allowed the angel Gabriel to descend from heaven and other devices allowed the Ascension of Christ to be most skilfully staged.

From the plans of a 12th–13th century French play about the Resurrection we learn that the plays were performed at different places in the church; at each place some form of platform or acting area was set, these often being called *mansions*. The Crucifix was placed in the east where the altar stood, with the sepulchre adjoining it on the north wall of the chancel; to the south was a gaol, followed by further mansions arranged down the nave of the church.

In the 12th century play 'Adam' there are descriptions of the mansions and costumes used. The Paradise was to be set up in a lofty place and hung around with curtains and silk hangings so that those within might be seen only from the shoulders up. There were to be sweet smelling flowers and trees with fruits hanging on them, so that it might seem a delectable place. The Saviour was to be clothed in a dalmatic—a priest's robe, whilst Adam was to have a red tunic and Eve a white garment and a white silk wimple. In some cases Paradise may well have been set up in the rood loft, that is, above the screen which separated the chancel from the nave.

Before long, however, the plays became too popular, their content too far removed from the simple Bible stories. The Church which had tended this new form of drama found it had got out of hand and the clergy were forbidden to take part. Performances were removed to the outside of the church and eventually to the market place or to other parts of the town. In England the performances were taken over by the Guilds who were responsible for a particular portion of each play. The plays were known as Mysteries, Miracles and Moralities; the Mystery and Miracle plays were made up of Bible stories and the Moralities showed virtues personified.

Although the plays had passed out from the church, in some towns the mansions were still arranged around an open place where temporary seating could be erected. You can see a somewhat similar arrangement of mansions in the drawing of the Valenciennes Mystery, in which they extend from Heaven on the left to Hell on the right. Incidentally, next time you go to the Pantomime notice that this arrangement still survives in one small feature, namely that the good

| Paradise | The Gate of | The Temple | The Gate of | Pilate's Palace | The Golden Gate | Limbo |
| A Hall | Nazareth | | Jerusalem | Prison under | Lake with Vessel | Hell |

The Mystery of the Passion, at Valenciennes, 1547

13

Medieval Angel (after a carving in the Beauchamp Chapel, Warwick)

fairy always enters from your left, while the demon king enters from the right.

Plans still exist showing a circular arrangement of these mansions; one can be seen in the manuscript of 'The Castle of Perseverance', and others exist in the scripts of the Cornish Mysteries which were probably performed in the amphitheatres at St. Just and Perranzabuloe. These performances were under the control of the Ordinary; he was a master of ceremonies whose duty was to see that the stage directions were carried out and to prompt the players, who were not expected to learn their parts.

Where the play was performed in different places around a town wheeled mansions, known as *pageants*, were used. These were waggons having an upper room or platform on which the actors performed, with a lower curtained area where they could dress. In addition they could act in the space surrounding the waggon hemmed in by the audience who stood around or were seated on specially erected scaffolds or perhaps in the windows of adjoining buildings.

The plays were presented with great attention to realistic detail, earthquakes, thunderbolts, miracles and fires were normal features, and the Mouth of Hell was constructed with massive jaws that opened and closed to permit the passage of many devils who prodded the damned into hell amid the smoke and flames which belched forth. The devils would run among the audience and play practical jokes on them: their costumes, and those of the angels who were often garbed in feathers, are sometimes found depicted in the churches, for when the Bible stories were being carved or painted the artists would naturally draw on the models that they had seen in the plays.

One or other of these forms of theatre provided the public with their drama throughout the Middle Ages and even beyond, and although they had ceased to

Devils at the mouth of Hell (after a wall painting in St. Michael's Church, St. Albans)

14

A medieval pageant

be organised by the Church they were, nevertheless performed on Church holidays.

THE RENAISSANCE IN ITALY

Up to the 13th century the Church had been largely responsible for thought and learning, but during the 14th century there came into being in Italy a rebirth of the ideas of the scholars of Ancient Greece and Rome. It soon became fashionable for a prince to surround himself with as many treasures of the Ancient World as he could lay hands on, manuscripts, statues and other relics, and to have about his court learned men, architects and artists who were authorities on the ancient ideas.

While the popular form of theatre continued to be enjoyed by the common people a different form came into being in the presentations staged at the courts or under the patronage of learned societies. One famous manuscript that had survived was that of the Ten Books of Architecture, by a Roman named

Performance of a play by Terence (after the Lyons Terence, 1493)

Vitruvius. Writing in the years 16–13 B.C., Vitruvius gave descriptions of civic buildings and in the fifth book dealt with theatres; the sections on typical Greek and Roman theatres include descriptions of the acoustics and scenery. He tells us that there were three kinds of scenes called the Tragic, Comic and Satyric; tragic scenes were delineated with columns, pediments, statues and other objects suited to kings; comic scenes exhibited private dwellings and satyric scenes were decorated with trees, caverns, mountains, and other rustic objects.

During the Renaissance many classical plays were discovered, notably those of Terence and Plautus, and attempts were made to present these in what was thought to be their original manner. Our best pictures of these performances can be seen in the illustrations to a publication of Terence's works known as the Lyons Terence. In these a simple platform stage is backed by curtained openings each representing the dwelling of the person named above the doorway, an arrangement reminiscent both of the medieval mansions arranged around the acting area and of the thyromata of the late Greek and Graeco-Roman theatres. As we saw earlier, a convention allowed the stage to be related to the 'house' at that moment revealed, so, although a change of scene could be represented merely by closing one curtain and opening another, the number of changes were limited and a great deal was left to the imagination of the audience.

SCENES AND MACHINES

At the beginning of the 15th century the perfection of the science of perspective

COLISEVS SI VE THEATRVM

*Stage for plays of Terence and Plautus.
The audience, viewed from the stage, with
practical mansions on either side*

mand a performance, generally a mixture of play, music, dance and spectacle.
An architect—at this time architects were
men of many capabilities usually receiv-
ing their early training as sculptors,
painters or in similar capacities—would
design the setting, the mechanical devices
and the seating for the spectators, who
were mostly courtiers but occasionally included members of the public.

One such architect was Sebastiano
Serlio who, in the second book of a treatise
on Architecture published in 1545, dealt
with perspective painting and included
much information on theatres. He attempted to find out the true nature of the
Roman theatre by studying the work of
Vitruvius and related these ideas to the
requirements of his own period. The
theatre shown here is similar to a Roman
theatre in that there are stepped seats
around a semi-circular orchestra facing a
wide stage, but this, unlike the Roman

provided a means of representing magni-
ficent scenes in a limited space, either
painted on canvas or solidly modelled.
The possibility of providing decorative,
realistic and later changeable backgrounds
was seized upon by the designers and thus
began the scenic movement which was to
lead to our modern picture-frame stage.

The earliest of the new theatres were
temporary structures, erected for a special
occasion and built in an existing great
hall. Each prince, attempting to outdo his
rivals, would, on the celebration of a
wedding or some other festivity, com-

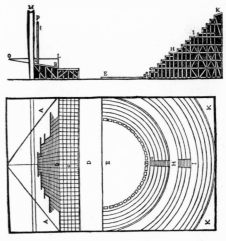

Plan and section of theatre by Serlio, 1545

17

stage, is not backed by a frons scenae but by a sloping stage on which scenery is mounted.

The scenery consisted of a number of angled panels standing, like open books, on either side of a vista leading to a background panel, the floor of the sloping stage being decorated with paving stones drawn in perspective. You will remember Vitruvius mentioned that the Roman stage had three kinds of settings, and Serlio includes his versions painted or built in perspective on his two-faced 'wings'. We should, however, be clear that the actors performed on the flat stage and that the scenic area was merely a background.

The problem of changing one scene into another occupied much of Serlio's time and takes up a great deal of space in a work written by Nicola Sabbattini in the first third of the seventeenth century called The Practice of Building Scenes and Machines. He described the methods used by the designers of the 16th century for presenting the many effects required by the *intermezzi*, an entertainment composed of prose, dance and scenic effects. He explained how to illuminate stage and auditorium with oil lamps and candles. He said it was customary to

arrange a number of oil lamps in a row of footlights across the front of the stage, but he does not recommend this practice as their smoke interferes with the view of the spectators, and the light blinds the actors and dancers. The auditorium lights were not dimmed as they are today, the theatre being lit by chandeliers which Sabbattini suggested should be lit simultaneously by fuses. His instructions, however, sound most dangerous when he speaks of spirit-soaked wicks and of candle-wax dripping on the audience.

From Sabbattini's book it is obvious that the Serlian type angle-wing was difficult to change. He suggests various methods of doing this, and some of them are illustrated here; however, by the time that Sabbattini was writing the flat wing had already replaced the angle-wing, thus making for easier changes.

Clouds had become an important part of Renaissance scenic decoration. At first cotton wool was applied to the ropes and poles which held the various machines; but later the clouds were of painted canvas on frames. Sabbattini gives various methods for building a sky over the stage while leaving spaces for machines to descend. He describes in detail how to cover part of the sky with clouds, and how to make a cloud descend with people in it, as well as many other effects and machines.

These scenic effects required a great deal of machinery, and if the illusion was to be complete this had to be hidden. Early in the development of the perspective scene two masking wings were arranged on either side at the front of the stage to hide the off-stage ends of the scenery, and when skies and clouds

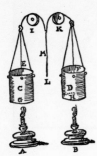

Stage lights (after Sabbattini)

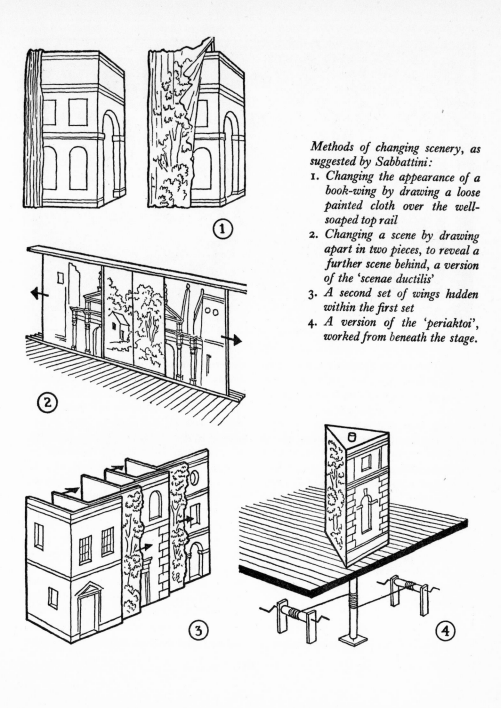

Methods of changing scenery, as suggested by Sabbattini:

1. *Changing the appearance of a book-wing by drawing a loose painted cloth over the well-soaped top rail*
2. *Changing a scene by drawing apart in two pieces, to reveal a further scene behind, a version of the 'scenae ductilis'*
3. *A second set of wings hidden within the first set*
4. *A version of the 'periaktoi', worked from beneath the stage.*

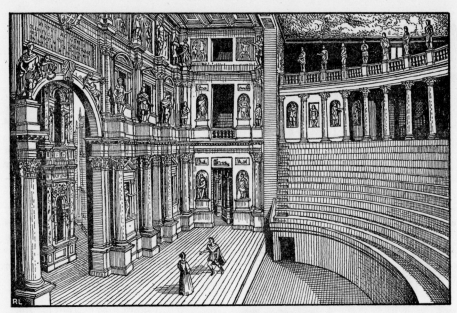

The Teatro Olimpico, Vicenza, 1580

became part of the scene a top piece was added which, together with the side wings, formed a decorative frontispiece. A front curtain was used with such a frame to hide the scene until the performance began; after that much of the scenic movement was intended to be seen and the curtain was not used again. Sabbattini, however, suggested that scenery could be changed unnoticed by the audience, if so required, by arranging for a trumpet to be blown at the back of the hall, or a rumour to be started that the staging of the rear seats was collapsing; he advised the use of the former, however, as the second suggestion might start a panic.

RENAISSANCE THEATRES IN ITALY

The court theatres had been temporary structures erected in the great hall or courtyard of a palace, but academic societies now began building permanent theatres. The most famous of these is the reconstruction of a Roman theatre designed by the architect Andrea Palladio, in 1580, for the Olympic Academy of Vicenza for their presentation of ancient plays. Palladio tried to build what he thought to be a correct Roman theatre according to the information given by Vitruvius and his own researches. Unlike the majority of Roman theatres, however, the Teatro Olimpico is built within a rectangular structure covered by a pitched roof. As the site was rather small Palladio was unable to design a semi-circular amphitheatre and orchestra but had to make them elliptical. The amphitheatre had tiers of seating rising to a colonnade corresponding to the Roman porticus. The seats faced a raised stage—the proscenae or proscenium area—which was backed by the frons scenae decorated with columns, niches and statues. There were five entries to this area, those in the side walls having balconies over. The ceiling over the stage was coffered whilst that over the auditorium is thought to have been painted to represent a velarium.

Behind the frons scenae is a further stage area with a sloping floor and a domed plaster ceiling painted to represent sky. Palladio died before the building was finished and it had to be completed by Vincenzo Scamozzi, who also designed the permanent scenery consisting of a number of streets of houses backing each of the openings.

These streets were built in perspective of timber and plaster, each street ending in a painted panel which extended the scene into the far distance. Both theatre and scenery still stand today and are used for yearly dramatic festivals.

Although this recreation of a Roman theatre greatly influenced the development of the playhouse, it is to other theatres that we must turn to find the true creations of the Renaissance, in that they served the courtly taste and allowed full use of the changeable perspective

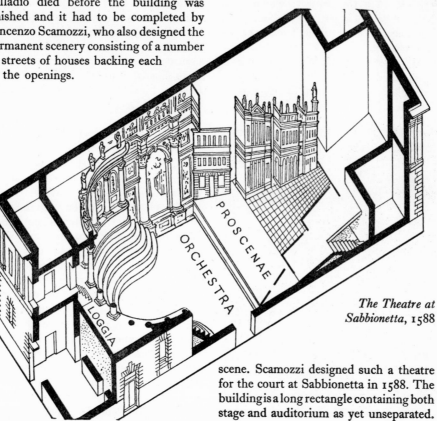

The Theatre at Sabbionetta, 1588

scene. Scamozzi designed such a theatre for the court at Sabbionetta in 1588. The building is a long rectangle containing both stage and auditorium as yet unseparated.

21

The stepped seats are arranged in a semi-circle around a slightly sloping orchestral area and both face a flat raised stage behind which is a sloping area where the scenery, designed in the Serlian manner, was set.

In many ways the imposing theatre built by Aleotti in the Farnese Palace at Parma in 1618 is similar to that of Sabbionetta, but here the orchestra was an elongated horse-shoe surrounded by a wall supporting the seats of the amphitheatre. Here, however, the scenic area is cut off by a frontispiece, which is no longer regarded as part of the scenery, but has become a permanent part of the architecture.

We must not think of these theatres as being used only for the performance of new plays or the revival of plays in the ancient manner; masques, with dancers, singers and theatrical extravagance in which the courtly personages took part, were often performed. The scenery provided a spectacular background and machinery enabled the royal persons to descend on cloud thrones and thence by steps to the orchestral area where they could lead the dancing. Pageant cars, monsters and like features were also introduced. One performance in 1628 was a mixture of drama, opera, tournament and marine spectacle. The visiting princes rode up into the theatre, the bridal couple sat in seats of honour facing the proscenium opening, gods and goddesses flew through the air and, the orchestral area having been flooded with water, monsters and islands with warriors on them floated into the hall where they fought. Finally the waters disappeared and the gods ascended into heaven.

THE ITALIAN COMEDY

While such spectacular performances were the rule at court, the public had their own theatres in the open streets where companies of players erected trestle platforms similar to those of Ancient Greece. On these were performed plays having stock situations and characters, the words being made up by each character as the play proceeded. This Italian comedy was known as the *Commedia dell'Arte*, many of the characters are well known to us: Columbine and Harlequin found their way into our pantomimes, and Punchinello exists as Mr. Punch. The actors wore characteristic clothing and small masks, and each played the same role all his life, improvising action and speeches to suit his individual character. Much of the comedy was very

The Farnese Theatre, Parma, 1618

The Commedia dell'Arte: Platform stage and actors (after Callot)

broad—the audience would laugh at the misfortune of a character who had a chamber-pot emptied over his head. The players deflated the pompous and made fun of the swaggering bully—the Capitano is a character very warlike and threatening until it comes to a fight, and the Doctor's learning is not so great as he would like to make out, his speeches being full of misquotations. The plays were fast and furious, dealing with situations familiar to the audience, who stood around the raised platform or leaned from their windows to share the fun.

This lively form of theatre was such a contrast to the courtly spectacles that it was inevitable that some prince, bored with formality, would turn his attention to this popular theatre and invite a company to his court. Gradually the popular comedians became fashionable and com-panies performed not only in the Italian courts but journeyed through Europe and appeared in France and England. Their theatre was most popular in France, and was destined to stimulate Molière to base his plays on their characters.

TUDOR ENGLAND

Although the Medieval drama was largely developed by the Guilds, it was natural that bands of professional players should eventually emerge from amongst the strolling minstrels and jongleurs. These troupes usually consisted of four men and a boy who played all the women's parts; for no woman was allowed to appear upon the English stage. They roamed the countryside performing wherever they obtained permission: in the halls of country houses, in guild halls and even in churches to which they gained admission under the claim of performing a miracle play. These players were under the protection of some lord and travelled as his servants; unless they had such protection they would quickly have found themselves in prison as rogues and vagabonds.

During the 16th century we find mention of many troupes under the patronage of lords and even royalty, but their life was far from easy. The changes brought about by the Reformation were keenly felt by the players whose plays, according to the authorities, often contained 'naughty and seditious matter.' The miracle plays, looked upon with favour by Queen Mary as upholding the Catholic faith, were in turn frowned upon by Protestant Elizabeth, and it was during the latter's reign that secular companies were formed.

When the actors performed in a hall they probably used the existing fittings. The typical medieval hall was entered through a passage called the 'screens', to one side of which were the pantries and kitchens, to the other the hall which was entered by two doors in the screen. At the opposite end of the hall was a raised dais with a table for the lord of the manor, in between were tables for the retainers. As the hall was high there was room above the screens for a gallery which could be used by musicians. When a performance was to be given the tables were drawn aside so that the players, using the pantries as a 'tiring house' or dressing rooms, could make their entry into the open space through the doors in the screen. If the play demanded the use of an upper level the gallery could be used.

Elizabethan performance in a medieval hall, before the screens

The early performances at the court of Henry VIII which may have been staged in this manner were called 'interludes'; it is not known precisely what this term means but it is generally thought to have applied to performances given at banquets or at other times when religious plays could not be performed. We do not know what scenery, if any, was used, but as various scenic elements were used in the guild plays, so similar features may well have been used here. There are instances where a trap door was required to allow an actor to appear from below, suggesting the need for some sort of raised platform. In the time of Elizabeth I mention is made of the use of mansions, which may have been similar to the medieval practical houses, or may perhaps have been influenced by the new Italian ideas.

As in Italy, so in England, the Universities began performing plays in the classical manner and making use of the Serlian arrangement of houses, and the court may well have been influenced by their example. Nevertheless, it would seem as though the inherent nature of the medieval stage continued as is suggested in the following quotation from Sir Philip Sydney's 'Defence of Poesie' (about 1584). "The Player, when he commeth in, must ever begin with telling where he is, or els the tale wil not be conceiued. Now ye shal haue three ladies walke to gather flowers, and then we must beleeue the stage to be a Garden. By and by, we heare newes of ship wracke in the same place, and then wee are to blame if we accept it not for a Rock. Vpon the backe of that, comes out a hidious Monster, with fire and smoke, and then the miserable beholders are bound to take it for a Caue. While in the meantime two capital armies flye in, represented with foure swords and bucklers, and then what harde heart will not receiue it for a pitched fielde?" He also mentions the use of notices to name the place of the stage or the function of a particular door.

THE SHAKESPEAREAN THEATRE

The performances to the general public were mainly given in town halls or inn yards. In the latter the players set up their platform and played to an audience standing about them or looking down from the open galleries surrounding the yard, but towards the end of the 16th century the authorities of the City of London became increasingly strict in their dealings with the players; finally one, James Burbage,

decided to build a theatre outside the City where his company would be free from restrictions. He chose Shoreditch and in 1576 built The Theatre in the open fields. This 'plaiehowse' proved so successful that Burbage built another close by called The Curtain: both his companies of players being under the protection of the Lord Chamberlain. Before long other theatres were built—the Newington Butts in Lambeth and, about 1587, The Rose, built by Philip Henslowe for the Lord Admiral's Men on the south bank of the Thames at Southwark.

A theatre which appears in some of the illustrated maps of the period is The Swan, built about 1594 in Southwark, and we also have a sketch of its interior which was copied by a Dutchman named Van Buchel from a drawing sent to him by his

The Swan (after de Witt)

25

friend de Witt on a visit to London. This shows three galleries ranged around an open yard, containing a raised rectangular stage backed by a tiring house. In his letter and sketch de Witt compares the Swan to a Roman theatre: he calls the tiring house *mimorum aedes* or house of the actors, the stage he terms the *proscenium* which means the area 'before the scenae', the lowest gallery the *orchestra*, that above the *sedilia* and above that the *porticus*. But although de Witt is comparing the building to a Roman theatre we must not think that the Elizabethan builders were necessarily trying to copy one, it is more likely they took its shape from the bull and bear baiting yards on the South Bank. (See picture, p. 27.)

The audience stood in the space around the stage called the 'yard', which was open to the sky and those who stood here were called 'groundlings'. By paying more you could sit in the galleries under cover. In the early days one of the galleries of the tiring house may have been used as a Lords' Room, where sat the gallants more desirous of being seen and showing off their finery than of seeing the play; this was later moved to a room to one side of the stage and the young gallants then sat on stools on the stage. (See frontispiece.)

On the stage are two large columns supporting a roof covering part of the stage, above this is a room on which the house flag is flying to show there will be a performance. Here there were machines for working simple effects, such as the lowering of the 'creaking throne' mentioned by Ben Jonson. The ceiling over the stage was called the 'heavens' and was brightly painted with the sun, moon and stars. The whole theatre was decorated in the new Italian manner, with columns painted to resemble marble, and other classical devices.

The front wall of the tiring house contains two double doors at stage level, above is a long open gallery divided by posts supporting the wall above. This is exactly what we should expect to find when we remember that the actors not only performed in these theatres, but toured the country where they performed in the halls against a similar backing of the screens. We know that even as late as 1603, a patent or licence was granted to the King's Players under the Great Seal of James I to Laurence Fletcher, William Shakespeare, Richard Burbage, and others and their associates, to play "comedies, tragedies, histories, enterludes, moralls, pastoralls, stage plaies, and such like" either at their usual house called The Globe, in Surrey, or "within anie towne Halls or moot-halls, or other convenient places" throughout his dominions.

Some scenery was used, as we can tell from the plays which were written to be performed in these theatres: a raised throne (*state*), a tent or a bed may have been brought on to the stage when needed, as suggested by the stage direction "a bed thrust out on the stage". Some stage directions suggest that trees were set up to represent a forest and we read of arbours, walls and tombs as items of scenery belonging to the players, and the use of ladders to reach the balconies. Trap doors allowed both players and scenery to ascend from, and descend to, the under-stage area which was used for hell; in most cases the stage stood high enough to permit movement beneath.

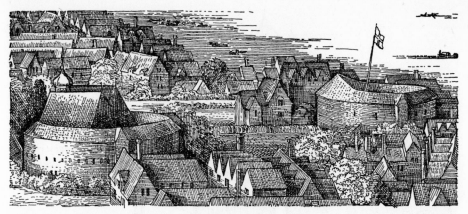

The second Globe Theatre (left) and the Bear Garden (right), after Hollar's 'Long View of London'

The stage was supported on posts or trestles, and curtains were hung around the sides to conceal the supports and under parts.

In addition to these open theatres there were a number of covered theatres, sometimes described as 'private theatres'. This term does not mean that the public were not admitted but probably applied to some method of payment enabling the owners to get around the regulations preventing the buildings being licensed as public theatres. One such was the Blackfriars, which was adapted from an existing hall in the Blackfriars monastery. This theatre was built for the Children of the Chapel Royal in 1576, but was taken over by James Burbage in 1596 and eventually became the winter quarters of the King's Men. Very little is known about the shape of these private theatres, in most cases they were small rectangular buildings perhaps fifty feet by one hundred feet in all. They had boxes and a tiring house, but exactly how these were arranged in relation to the stage is not known.

Towards the end of the century more theatres were built; probably the best known was The Globe where so many of Shakespeare's plays were first performed. This was built in 1599 by the sons of James Burbage, and much of the timber from The Theatre was used in its construction. It was destroyed by fire in 1613 during the performance of Shakespeare's 'Henry VIII'. According to Sir Henry Wotton the whole house burnt to the ground in less than an hour "yet nothing did perish but wood or straw, and a few forsaken cloaks; only one man had his breeches set on fire that would perhaps have broiled him if he had not by the benefit of a provident wit put it out with a bottle of ale".

The Globe was rebuilt in 1614 in an even grander manner as may be guessed from the illustration of the exterior which shows the building over the stage to be a much finer affair than that in de Witt's drawing, and it is only fair to assume that

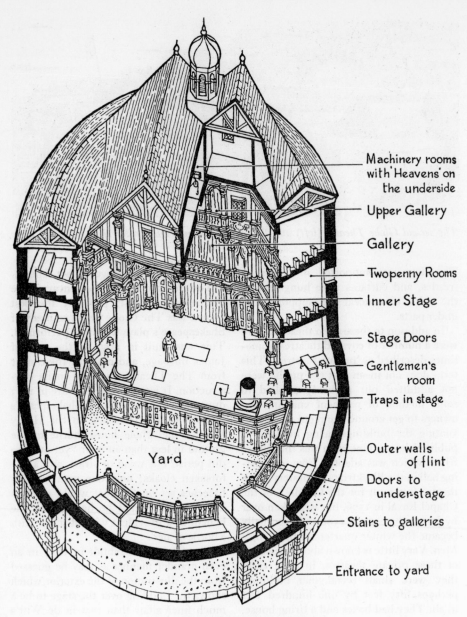

Machinery rooms
with 'Heavens' on
the underside

Upper Gallery

Gallery

Twopenny Rooms

Inner Stage

Stage Doors

Gentlemen's
room

Traps in stage

Outer walls
of flint

Doors to
under-stage

Stairs to galleries

Entrance to yard

Yard

The second Globe Theatre (1614)

the tiring house and stage had also developed in the years since the Swan was built. From the plays written for the later theatres it would appear that a third door, or opening, had been introduced into the tiring house façade, and this seems to have been curtained. Within this opening some of the indoor scenes could have been performed. It is also possible that the open gallery above had been rearranged to include both a gallery and windows, and some people think a third gallery was introduced above this. However, just how these various features were arranged is not known, many intelligent guesses have been made and you will see many reconstructions: our own attempt is shown opposite.

Two other open theatres belong to this period—The Hope and The Fortune. The first reminds us that the actors had to compete with bulls and bears: built on the site of the original Bear Garden, the contract for this theatre stipulates that the heavens over the stage must be built without posts so that the stage could be removed for the bull and bear baiting, in other respects the theatre was to be like the Swan. The contract for the Fortune tells us that this theatre was to be built foursquare instead of round, and that its stage and tiring house were to be similar to those at the Globe, except that the stage was to be boarded in around its edges. We know from the prologue spoken by the Fortune players when they moved to the Red Bull, one of the covered theatres, in 1640, that the former theatre had at least one curtained opening.

These then are some of the theatres for which Marlowe, Shakespeare and Jonson wrote, and you can read more about them,

Early 17th century stage (after title-page of the play 'Roxana')

the plays, the players and the companies of children in the companion Outline *Shakespeare and His Plays*. The theatres continued in use on and off until 1642 when the Puritans finally closed them all. The actors were scattered and many of the playhouses destroyed; until the Restoration in 1660 there was little theatrical activity.

COURT MASQUES

In 1656 Sir William Davenant managed to stage 'The Siege of Rhodes' at his own house, by claiming that it was not a play but a 'Declamation with Musick after the manner of the Ancients'. Although Davenant staged one or two such

29

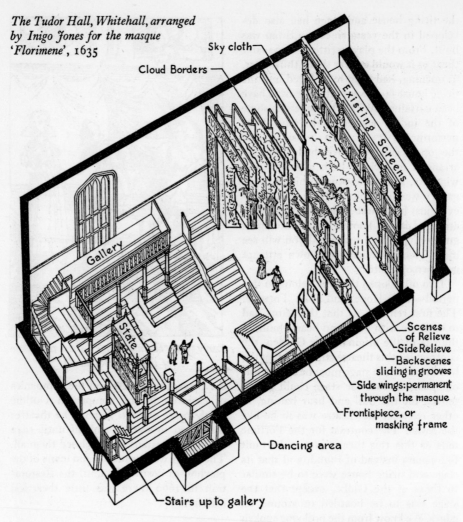

The Tudor Hall, Whitehall, arranged by Inigo Jones for the masque 'Florimene', 1635

Sky cloth

Cloud Borders

Existing Screens

Gallery

State

Scenes of Relieve
Side Relieve
Backscenes sliding in grooves
Side wings: permanent through the masque
Frontispiece, or masking frame

Dancing area

Stairs up to gallery

private shows in spite of Puritan objections it was not until the Restoration in 1660 that the theatres were officially allowed to re-open; when this took place the old style open playhouse had gone for ever to be replaced by indoor theatres. These were adapted to allow the use of the perspective scenery, developed before the Commonwealth in the court masques by such men as Inigo Jones. He had travelled in Italy, visited the Teatro Olimpico, and brought back many of the Italian scenic ideas.

During the early years of the 17th

A court masque

century the Masques at Court were arranged in much the same manner as for the interludes at the court of Elizabeth I, various items of scenery being placed around the acting area so that many places were represented at one and the same time. The new methods of using changeable scenery, however, required that only one scene could be visible at any one time.

'The Masque of Blackness', produced in 1605 by Ben Jonson and Inigo Jones, made early but simple use of the new scenic ideas: on the removal of a cloth painted to represent a landscape, a sea-scene with moving waves and 'the descent of night' was revealed. In the same year Inigo Jones went to Oxford to stage the academic play and for this he experimented with a background of periaktoi; these, turned together, showed three complete pictures. In other productions he used side wings, painted front and back, which, when rotated about a central post, showed a new scene.

The court masques were staged in a hall adapted as a theatre, nearly half the hall being occupied by a raised stage for scenes and machines. (See pp. 30–1.) Opposite, at the correct viewing point for the perspective scene, was set the state; between this and the stage was a dancing area connected to the latter by steps or ramps. Ranged around the state on one or more levels were stepped seats—*degrees* —for the courtiers and ambassadors. You can see all these in the drawing showing the arrangements for the presentation of 'Florimene' in 1635. Behind a decorative frame are four pairs of Serlian wings, backed by flat 'shutters' which pulled apart in grooves to reveal further shutters or a distant scene set before a painted skycloth. In this design the side wings were not changed, but by 1640 we find that Jones was more ambitious, his drawings for 'Salmacida Spolia' being annotated 'ye scaene doe altogither change with ye back shutters'. For this he replaced the Serlian wings by several sets of flat wings arranged to slide in grooves set parallel with the front of the stage.

Jones also designed the costumes which were both varied and imaginative. He introduced ideas based on the Italian Comedy and many designs were based on Oriental and Indian costumes. The heroic masquers had costumes based partly on classical designs and partly on the fashionable costumes of the period; some of these appear in our drawing of a Court Masque.

RESTORATION PLAYHOUSES

The spectacles made possible by this movable scenery could not be ignored when new theatres were built after the Restoration. Many companies were formed but these were quickly limited to two; these were the King's Men and the Duke's Men, and by their charters or patents they were permitted to perform plays and were also empowered to engage women to perform in their theatres. At first they used the theatres which had survived the Puritan purge; whilst the Duke's Men under Davenant used The Cockpit and later Salisbury Court, the King's Men under Killigrew used a converted tennis court[1] in Vere Street, sometimes called the Theatre Royal, which opened in 1660.

[1] A tennis court at this time was a rectangular roofed building similar to that which still exists at Hampton Court.

The King's Company moved in 1663 to the first of the Theatres Royal to be built on the present site, between Bridges Street and Drury Lane. We have no illustration of this building, but a visitor to England described it as "nearly of a circular form, surrounded in the inside by boxes separated from each other, and divided into several rows of seats, for the greater accommodation of the ladies and gentlemen, who, in conformity with the freedom of the country, sit together indiscriminately; a large space being left on the ground floor for the rest of the audience. The scenery is very light, capable of a great many changes, and embellished with beautiful landscapes". Samuel Pepys thought the building to have "some faults . . . as the narrowness of the passages in and out of the pitt, and the distance from the

The Duke's Theatre, Dorset Gardens (after the Crown copyright original in the Victoria and Albert Museum)

stage to the boxes, which I am confident cannot hear". He also says that the musicians were at first placed below but were later moved to the upper regions. Pepys was in the theatre on May Day, 1668, for he records "a disorder in the pitt by its raining in, from the cupola at the top, it being a very foul day and cold".

In 1661 Davenant also converted a tennis court, known as Lisle's Tennis Court, into the Lincoln's Inn Fields Playhouse, but he soon became dissatisfied and in 1671 the company moved to the Dorset Gardens Theatre, which is supposed to have been designed for them by Sir Christopher Wren. Drawings of this theatre show a stage flanked by two doors on either side, above which were balconies: these doors were used by the actors for entering the stage as were those of the classical and later of the Elizabethan stage, the difference being that here they were at the sides to make way for a high opening through which the scenery could be viewed; above this was a gallery used by the musicians.

The Duke's Theatre, Dorset Gardens

Part of the audience was seated in a pit, surrounded on three sides by two levels each of seven boxes, above which was some form of open gallery, the whole being elaborately decorated with statuary, carvings and gilding, and lit by numerous candles. The balconies over the doors of entry could be used either by the actors or the audience. Although, today, we call the opening between the stage and auditorium the 'proscenium opening', the

The Theatre Royal, Drury Lane, designed by Wren, 1674

either side of the stage, but when Sir Christopher Wren built the second Theatre Royal in 1674 he provided only two doors on either side. This theatre was not so ornate as the Dorset Gardens Theatre. A section drawn by Wren is generally accepted as being for this theatre

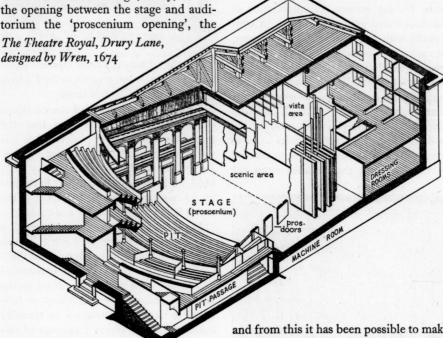

vista area

scenic area

DRESSING ROOMS

STAGE
(proscenium)

pros. doors

PIT

MACHINE ROOM

PIT PASSAGE

whole of the forward stage of the Restoration theatre with its doors of entry, and in some cases its own ceiling or heaven, was still known by the correct classical title of 'proscenium', or 'area before the scenae'; so we find the doors of entry referred to as 'proscenium doors'.

The first Theatre Royal in Bridges Street had three proscenium doors on

and from this it has been possible to make our reconstruction. The main acting area was in the auditorium, the side walls of which, containing both boxes and proscenium doors, splayed out to form a fan-shaped pit. This had a sloping floor and benches which followed the curve of the stage front. Three amphitheatres, or galleries, faced the stage, the lower being divided by low rails into separate boxes of which the centre was the royal box.

The Corinthian pilasters of the side walls were built in perspective and from the king's seat would have appeared to continue the scenic vista. Behind the acting area at least half the building was given over to a scenic area, with dressing rooms flanking a space allowing extra depth for special vistas. Beneath was space for the scenic machinery; this could be reached either from the stage or from the passages under the side boxes leading to the pit.

In the main the audience at these theatres were from the court, and consisted largely of the fops and beaux with their court-ladies and fashionable courtesans. Their manners and behaviour left much to be desired; they were forever chatting, flirting or even fighting. The habit of sitting on the stage still continued, and the actors often had to fight their way through a crowd. In our view from the stage of Drury Lane some members of the audience can be seen on the stage to the right of the picture, while one gentleman addresses the crowd from before the lower proscenium door.

The actresses, like Mrs. Bracegirdle and Nell Gwyn, had now gained positions of importance in the companies. The normal fashionable clothes were mainly worn, but the conventions introduced by Inigo Jones still persisted for heroic, classical and oriental characters. The plays which pleased this fashionable society were those of artifice, wit and immorality, and were written by such men as Dryden, Congreve, Wycherley and Sir John Vanbrugh.

In 1682 the two companies were merged into one at the Theatre Royal, Drury Lane, under the control of Christopher Rich. He made several changes to the theatre all directed to making more money by packing in larger audiences. Under Rich the old system by which the company had shared the profits was superseded by the payment of salaries. The older actors soon became dissatisfied with Rich's mean and grasping management, and they broke away and formed a new company under Thomas Betterton, who had been licensed to run a theatre, and in 1695 they moved into the theatre in Lincoln's Inn Fields. Life proved little better for them here, and soon both theatres were turning to all sorts of expedients to draw the public, drama taking a back seat to any sort of capers.

Their theatre was small and inconvenient and eventually Betterton made over his licence to Vanbrugh, who built a new playhouse which he designed in the French manner with tiers of boxes arranged in a horse-shoe around the pit. This playhouse was built in the Haymarket in the grand manner usually associated with Vanbrugh's architectural work. Because of its size the company were not much more successful here, and eventually the playhouse was used as an Opera House; even then it was not a success.

One of Rich's alterations to Wren's Theatre Royal, made in 1696, was to cut back the stage by some four feet and replace the lower proscenium doors by boxes for the audience; by this means he started a movement which was to push the actor from the stage amid the audience, back into the scenic area, thus allowing the size of the pit to be increased. Rich was thoroughly disliked and eventually lost his Patent to the Theatre in 1709; it was taken over by a group of

Wren's Theatre Royal, Drury Lane; view from the stage

actor managers. Meanwhile Rich took over the Lincoln's Inn theatre, but died before he could re-open it. This was left to his son John, who, to draw the public, invented the English pantomime, which was based on various fantasies woven around the character of Harlequin. These pantomimes were highly successful and Rich played the part of Harlequin. In 1727 he put on a musical production which was to be an even greater success and took the town by storm, this was 'The Beggar's Opera', by John Gay.

THE GEORGIAN THEATRE

In 1732 John Rich moved from his Lincoln's Inn theatre to a new building designed by Edward Shepherd and built in Covent Garden. In this theatre the proscenium area included only one door and stage box a side. Three tiers of boxes enclosed a fan-shaped pit with further boxes opposite the stage at the bottom level, above these were two galleries which, though similar in their arrangement to those at Drury Lane, followed the current movement by being much larger. The benched pit was now separated from the stage by an enclosed area for the musicians.

The theatre opened with Congreve's 'Way of the World' and was followed by a revival of 'The Beggar's Opera'. It was here that Peg Woffington appeared and played, amongst other parts, the male role in 'The Constant Couple'. Later she played at Drury Lane, where Garrick became famous. He made his first successful appearance at a little theatre in Goodman's Fields, for although only Covent Garden and Drury Lane were licenced to perform plays, numerous other theatres were opening during the 18th century. These unlicenced theatres got around the restrictions on their performing plays in various ingenious ways. Samuel Foote was to invite his friends to take a cup of tea and watch his actors in training at the Little Theatre in the Haymarket, and Garrick's first appearance at Goodman's Fields was billed as 'A Concert of Vocal and Instrumental Musick, divided into two parts. Between the two parts will be presented an Historical play called the Life and Death of King Richard III'. The two patent, or licenced, theatres were jealous of their rights and the success which Garrick's performances brought to this theatre made them bring an action to have the theatre closed.

Garrick eventually became part manager of Drury Lane; here he made many innovations, among them the introduction of "order, decency and decorum", and the use of patent oil lamps to light the scenery. Probably his most important move was to clear the audience from the stage, and from the Green Room where society gathered to meet the actresses. From descriptions written later it would seem that the audience on the stage was not confined to a few persons seated on chairs, but provision was made for numerous persons by building raised seats in front of the boxes and even the proscenium doors; in at least one instance, an amphitheatre of raised seats was built around the rear of the stage and boxed in with "dirty worn out scenery"; seated here the heads of the audience reached the scenic clouds.

However, if the audience were to be removed from the stage they had to be accommodated elsewhere, so in 1762 the old theatre was once again enlarged. We do not know what these alterations were, but we do know about the major alteration carried out in 1775 by Robert Adam. On the stage there was now only one proscenium door, with boxes over, on either side, the stage front had been cut back to a straight line and an orchestra pit separated it from the audience: this was a place for the musicians and must not be confused with the earlier orchestras of Greece and Rome. Although he retained the walls enclosing Wren's pit up to stage level, he removed the heavy Corinthian pilasters and replaced them by light posts, which allowed him to introduce a third tier of boxes on either side. Instead of the heavy plaster decorations he painted apple-green and gold decorations on the flat fronts of the boxes. The lower level of boxes facing the stage remained much the same, but the two upper galleries were extended to the back wall of the old building and included the area formally occupied by stairs and foyers, which were probably rehoused in a new addition fronting on Drury Lane.

There is a drawing showing the redesigned interior in the book 'The Works of Robert and James Adam', but you must be careful when you look at this view because Robert Adam made the theatre appear larger by drawing the people in it half their proper size; actually it was quite a small building.

The theatre underwent one more change when it was redecorated in 1783 by Capon, the resident scene designer. From the Adam drawing and one by Capon it can be seen that the auditorium was still lit by candles in wall brackets, chandeliers being hung over the stage.

During the 18th century, the audiences were changing from the courtly society of the Restoration; the Quality still attended but now middle class tradesmen had joined them, and the upper galleries were filled with servants and lackeys. This new audience introduced a moralising and sentimental element into the plays. The two great dramatists of the late 18th century were Goldsmith, with his comedy 'She Stoops to Conquer', and Sheridan who wrote 'The School for Scandal'. Our illustration shows the famous screen scene from the latter play as performed at Adam's Drury Lane. This shows that the scenery had not changed to any great extent: side wings were used, joined overhead by borders and backed by shutters or 'flats' which, being in two parts, could be drawn off to either side behind the wings to reveal another set of shutters directly behind, or a deeper area of stage enclosed by further wings, borders and flats. Most interior scenes were represented in this way, the doors and windows being painted on the wings, the actors—now pushed back amid the scenery—making their entries between the wings. This cannot have looked very realistic but in the exterior scenes a nearer approach to realism could be made, and Garrick helped these effects by replacing the hanging chandeliers by lights concealed behind the wings and borders.

During Garrick's management of Drury Lane the scene designer was de Loutherbourg. He used flats painted in perspective with openings cut in them to reveal further flats in turn cut to show a painted background. In addition to these standard units, cut-out pieces of scenery were placed across the stage and reality

The Theatre Royal, Drury Lane, as altered by Robert Adam, 1775: a performance of 'The School for Scandal'

was heightened by building ramps, steps and different levels of platforms behind these 'cut-outs' and 'ground-rows'. These designs were created for the spectacular productions that now gained importance. For 'The Wonders of Derbyshire, or Harlequin in the Peak' he made studies of the Derbyshire scenery, and as many people came to see his settings as came to see the plays. He experimented with various ways of illuminating the stage and used gauzes and transparencies. So we see the stage scene gradually beginning to change from the formal arrangement of side wings, flats and borders which changed in full view of the audience, to these 'set-pieces' whose setting on the stage needed to be hidden from the audience. These scenes were set behind a shallow down-stage scene, the flats of which masked the movement of stage hands behind.

LARGER THEATRES

By 1791 it was decided to rebuild Drury Lane and Garrick commissioned Henry Holland to design the new building which was opened in 1794. In place of the small playhouse, which had been typical of English theatres, this theatre was by comparison enormous, with five tiers of boxes and a much enlarged pit of horse-shoe form; two tiers of boxes faced the stage, with one large and deep circle above and a gallery higher still. When first opened there were no proscenium doors,

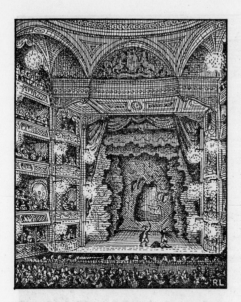

The third Theatre Royal, Drury Lane, designed by Henry Holland, 1794

the small 'fore-stage' being bounded by boxes. However, the day of the proscenium doors was not yet over and they were later introduced into this building by extending the walls of the auditorium onto the stage.

Because the stage structure and scenery were largely built of wood and canvas, and the lighting was either by candles or oil lamps, there was a great danger of fire. In an attempt to offset this a great curtain of sheet-iron cut off the stage from the auditorium; in addition, four tanks were installed over the auditorium to provide the water necessary for fire-fighting. In spite of these precautions, however, the theatre burnt to the ground in 1809, when the tanks did great damage by falling into the pit. At the time of the fire the theatre was under the management of Sheridan, the playwright.

Drury Lane was not alone in the trend towards larger theatres. In 1784 Covent Garden was enlarged, but the result was not satisfactory and in 1791 it was altered again, this time by Holland who once more built the boxes around a horse-shoe pit. The lower tier directly surrounding the pit was divided by low partitions into separate boxes. The benches had hinged pieces fitting across the gangways, and these could be lowered to seat more people—when you were in, you were in, and you had to stay or climb out over the audience. There was still a proscenium door on each side of the stage with a box over it, and a separate box was partitioned off from the stage end of each tier of galleries, the stage projecting forward to embrace them. The proscenium doors were flanked by pilasters supporting a ceiling over the projecting stage, the whole unit forming a kind of frame to the opening. In front of the stage was an orchestra pit separated from the audience by a low partition topped with metal spikes. These were a feature of most theatres as the audiences were not well behaved, and there were many riots throughout the 18th and 19th centuries. Usually these started when the management tried to increase the price of seats, but at other times the audience might take offence at some actor or manager, or at the manner of performance, or simply out of drunkenness. Sometimes they would content themselves with throwing orange peel or bottles at the stage or pennies at the chandeliers, but at other times in more serious mood swords and cudgels were drawn and seats and benches thrown around. If the crowd got onto the stage

The 'Old Price' riot at Covent Garden Theatre, 1809

itself they would break up the scenery, unless they happened to fall down the stage traps which the management left open for this purpose. Once or twice the audience completely wrecked the theatre, and sometimes the riots would continue night after night. The celebrated Old Price Riots which took place at Covent Garden in 1809 went on for sixty-seven nights.

THE PROVINCIAL THEATRES

Although London was the centre of theatrical activity the Provinces were not neglected. In Elizabethan days London companies had toured the country, and companies of strolling players performed in towns and cities, in various buildings adapted for the purpose. Eventually playhouses were built in the principal cities and towns. The remains of such a theatre can be seen in Orchard Street, Bath; this was built in 1750 and by 1768 it had received a Royal Patent which entitled it to be called the Theatre Royal. It was fitted, as we should expect with boxes, or galleries, in three tiers surrounding a rectangular pit. At the same time as this theatre was erected in Bath, similar buildings were being built all over the country, although in most the three tiers were normally reduced to two. In Leicester a Mr John Bass received permission from the Corporation on the 9th February, 1750, to erect a building called at first The Assembly Rooms, but afterwards known as the Old Playhouse. This is described as having been "fitted up with boxes, pit and gallery", and it is further recorded that the great actress

Strolling players on the move (after Theodore Lane)

Mrs Siddons appeared here with her husband in 1778.

These theatres were built and run by managers whose companies made a regular circuit of towns and villages in their area; in the larger towns they built proper theatres, but in the smaller places they made do with some hall or barn. The players walked from town to town, often carrying their goods and scenery on their backs, but more usually the equipment would be carried in a cart with the ladies and children of the company riding on top.

At Bristol the earliest theatre was built in 1729, but the oldest of these provincial theatres which is still in use today is their Theatre Royal, built in 1764 in spite of opposition from the puritan element, who were afraid that the theatre would "diffuse an habit of idleness, indolence and debauchery throughout this once industrious city". The building today has undergone many alterations. The archi-tect was John Paty, who obtained plans of Wren's Drury Lane from the resident carpenter. The overall size of the Bristol theatre is comparable with this building, and the back-stage areas have the same arrangement of a 'vista' stage set between dressing rooms. One period feature which remains is the 'thunder run' above the auditorium ceiling; here a number of cannon balls are allowed to bang and bounce their way along a wooden track, shaking the very structure on their journey.

The Georgian Theatre built at Richmond in Yorkshire, in 1788, is an example of the theatres which were erected in the smaller towns visited by the circuit companies. The Yorkshire circuit was under the control of Samuel Butler, and included Harrogate, Richmond, Kendal, Ripon, Northallerton and Beverley. The company flourished but eventually some towns were lost to other circuits, and the Butler company broke off their connections with the theatre in 1830. After this it was used only infrequently until in 1848 the building ceased to be used as a theatre. The pit was removed and a new floor was built at stage level, the area underneath being converted into wine cellars. Today, these have been removed and the pit has been replaced, reached by a passage under the side boxes in the same manner as at Drury Lane. It is enclosed by boxes with a gallery above and seats over the side boxes. A small orchestra pit is entered from the pit passage. Here too are the proscenium doorways with boxes over, used either by the actors or the public. In the stage floor are traps which were worked from the machine room under the front half of the stage, at the back are two stairways leading down to the dressing rooms. The stage is built on a rake or slope; this is a feature of all these theatres and is a relic of the early perspective stages.

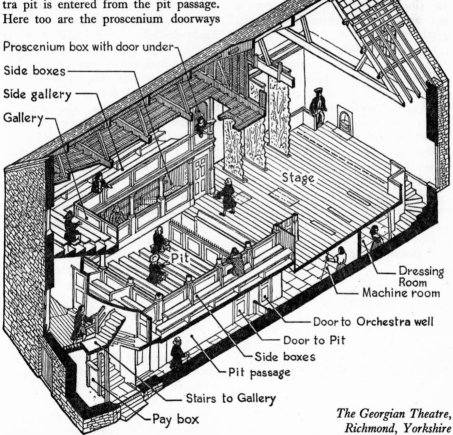

Proscenium box with door under
Side boxes
Side gallery
Gallery
Stage
Pit
Dressing Room
Machine room
Door to Orchestra well
Door to Pit
Side boxes
Pit passage
Stairs to Gallery
Pay box

The Georgian Theatre, Richmond, Yorkshire

Where other circuit theatres remain today, although at opposite ends of the country, their size and arrangement are practically identical. Some, however, instead of being rectangular have a horseshoe shaped pit and this arrangement can be seen in the theatres on the Fisher circuit in East Anglia, at Beccles, Bungay and North Walsham. These theatres, built in the 1820's, were similar to that at Portsmouth which was the habitat of that most memorable of theatrical managers, Mr Vincent Crummles, whose story is told by Charles Dickens in 'Nicholas Nickleby'.

Toward the middle of the 19th century most of the circuits disintegrated and many theatres closed down, the fittings were sold and the buildings converted to other uses. Usually the pit, boxes and gallery were pulled out and the whole floored over at stage level to make a 'useful' hall. Many such shells remain today: the Bungay theatre is now a laundry, that at North Walsham a church hall.

Perhaps there is an old theatre in your town! Why not try to find it? Your local library will have copies of early directories, and in these you will find a short description of the important buildings in each town. From this you will learn if there was a theatre and if so where it was. Look under the street lists and you will be able to find the position of the building in the street, then see if it still stands. The description may be like this from Kelly's Post Office Directory for Leicester, 1848: "The Theatre, a pretty and compact building situated in Horsefair Street, is open at the Races and occasionally at other periods. Lessee, Charles Gill". Or you may find your information in early guide books such as A Descriptive and Historical Guide to Ashby-de-la-Zouch, published by T. Wayte, 1831, where we read "The Theatre, Bath Street, was built in 1828, by Mr. Bennett, the manager of the Worcester company. It is neatly fitted up with boxes, gallery and pit. Mr. Bennett's company attend Ashby during the summer months. The house will hold about £50". Today this building still stands, but at first sight appears bare of any theatrical traces; only a close investigation reveals the sloping stage still in place beneath a later flat floor, while marks and painting on the walls show where boxes, gallery and stairs once stood.

Here is a chance for you to be a real and useful investigator. Perhaps you can find an old forgotten theatre that is still more or less intact. Whatever you find the authors will be pleased to hear from you if you write to them at the publisher's address about your find.

The companies timed their arrival at a place on their circuit with some local event, such as the week of the races, or when the militia were in town. The actors arrived with a roll of drums and visited the local gentry to gain their

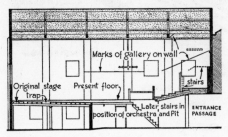

Remains of Theatre (1828) *at Ashby-de-la-Zouch*

An eighteenth-century Provincial Theatre

'The Benefit Night' (*after a drawing in 'The Life of an Actor'*)

patronage. Each principal actor would have a Benefit Night, and it was his job to gain a patron among the local big-wigs. The patron chose the play to be performed on that evening and, it was hoped, persuaded his friends to buy tickets and fill the boxes. It could be a hard and difficult life as you can see from the picture of a Benefit Night, and at times it could be very humiliating. The actors had their revenge, however, when the audience was particularly rustic; in one instance they made a point of answering each other with speeches from different plays so that the whole performance made complete nonsense, but they were nevertheless received with great applause. These strolling players did not die out entirely and, until the present century stock-companies continued to roam the country with their fit-up stages which they erected at country fairs.

The amount of scenery depended on the financial resources of the company, usually there were a number of stock wings and borders which were used for interior or exterior scenes; no one would be very particular about their use, and one interior was as good as another for most plays. Where a stage was not sufficiently wide to draw off the two parts of the back-flats, cloths were used instead; these were fixed to a roller and could be rolled or unrolled by pulling on a cord.

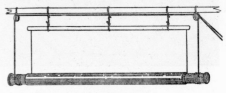

A roller cloth

Usually there was a scenic artist with the company, and he would touch up the permanent scenes or make special items. There was no attempt as yet at the sort of realism seen on our present-day stage, where whole settings are built to suit the needs of each play.

THE STAGE MACHINE

In the larger provincial theatres we can see how the scenery was used, and how the larger stages were specially built for the purpose. Although the scenic arrangements remained basically the same as in Restoration times, the whole stage area had by now become more or less standard as a machine for changing scenery. If you look on page 50 you will see a reconstruction of the Theatre Royal, Plymouth, designed by John Foulston in 1811, which shows how this machinery was arranged. Although not shown in this drawing it was usual for the whole of the central area of the stage to be made so that it could open in sections. Until 1947 the Theatre Royal, Leicester, had much of this under-stage equipment in position and our plan shows the bridges, traps and some

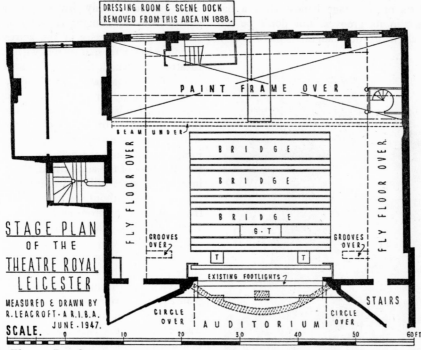

The Theatre Royal, Leicester, 1836, showing narrow sloat cuts and wider bridge cuts. Note the two corner traps (T) and the wider grave trap (GT). The original curved front to the stage is clearly shown

47

narrower sections, known as 'sloat cuts', which could be drawn aside to allow a single piece of scenery to be raised.

All this equipment could be made to work at the same time; at a given signal the wings would be drawn off to reveal a new set, the borders would change, ground-rows rose through the stage together with a group of actors on a bridge, like those in our drawing of the backstage of a Victorian Theatre (p. 57). Perhaps we are today too used to the realistic changes accomplished by films and television, and we might laugh at the creaking, groaning bridges or the frantic efforts of the stage hands when a flat stuck in its grooves. But don't be too quick with your laughter, there was a great deal of the true make-believe and let's-pretend in these scene changes, which is at heart the very essence of 'Theatre'.

As the stage had to open in so many separate parts, a great many timber posts were needed to support the stage joists, and provide guides and supports for the bridges, traps and sloats. Indeed there was a veritable forest of timber under the stage, which made a very bad fire risk. In the early 1800's gas replaced the oil lamps and candles, but, although this made the control of lighting easier, it did not help in reducing fire risks. The gas flames were protected only by simple wire guards from the hanging canvas scenery and the gauze dresses of the actresses. Needless to say there were many dreadful theatre fires, which account for the very strict precautions that are taken today.

In his design for the Theatre Royal, Plymouth, Foulston attempted to combat these difficulties by building a dividing wall between the stage and the auditorium, and by using the new cast-iron for the structure of the auditorium. Proscenium doors were still a feature of this building, but without the balcony above; they led onto the front area of the stage which, since the whole area of stage was used by the actors, must now be called the fore-stage, although this was once the stage proper. The auditorium had completely changed from the old rectangular plan and the two tiers of boxes enclosed a circular pit; unlike earlier examples this was entered at the back, through a door beneath the first tier of boxes. Here we can see the beginnings of a movement which led, during the first quarter of the century, to the raising of the boxes

Scene-painters (after 'Life of an Actor')

48

sufficiently high for the pit to extend outwards beneath them, the raised boxes taking the name which Foulston gave to the first tier, 'The Dress Circle of Boxes'. Above the boxes a large gallery faced the stage, while the side areas at this level were known as the 'slips'. Each part of the auditorium had its own coffee rooms or saloons, where the audience could gather in the intervals or before the play.

FRAMES, PICTURES AND SPECTACLES

The general tendency during the 19th century was for larger theatres, with increased seating and larger profits for the managements. The earlier small playhouses had permitted subtlety of acting, but these larger theatres forced the actors to adopt broader actions and louder voices if they were to be seen or heard in the far recesses; as a result it was hardly surprising that the tendency was for spectacular visual productions.

Holland's Theatre Royal, Drury Lane, was burnt down in 1809 and when rebuilt in 1812 to the designs of James Wyatt it seated some 1280 persons. Covent Garden too was destroyed by fire in 1808, and this was greatly increased in size when it was rebuilt to the designs of Smirke. It was as a result of the change in prices of admission to cover the cost of rebuilding this theatre that the Old Price Riots broke out. Covent Garden was now the home of pantomimes staged in a spectacular and sensational manner, one such production including an elephant.

The shape of the theatre had, however, changed very little and the proscenium doors and boxes were still in use. At Drury Lane, although the doors had been brought back into use in the previous building, they were omitted from the new theatre and two large decorative lamps stood before the place where they should have been; but these lights distracted the attention of the audience and they were removed, to be replaced for a short while by the proscenium doors. There were boxes above the lamps which were flanked by pilasters, and the actual stage opening was enclosed by massive Corinthian columns with gilt capitals supporting an arched ceiling over the fore-stage. Writing of this theatre W. J. Lawrence tells us "for the old fashioned proscenium arch was substituted a gilded picture frame, remote from the footlights, over which the actors were forbidden to step. Grumblings both loud and deep were heard among the players over the various deprivations, and finally, old Dowton, pluckier than the rest, broke into open rebellion, 'Don't tell me of frames and pictures!' he exclaimed, with choler, 'If I can't be heard by the audience in the frame I'll walk out of it.' And out of it he came!"

The move to make the actors part of the scenic picture was not popular with them, and it must certainly have been something of a trial that they were not to use the fore-stage. Under the circumstances, however, the change was inevitable and by the middle of the century most large theatres had finally done away with the proscenium doors. When the Haymarket Theatre built by Nash in 1820, was altered in 1843, the management proudly advertised "During the recess the Theatre has undergone extensive alterations: the proscenium has been entirely remodelled, and the whole of the interior decorated in a most costly and (continued on page 52)

49

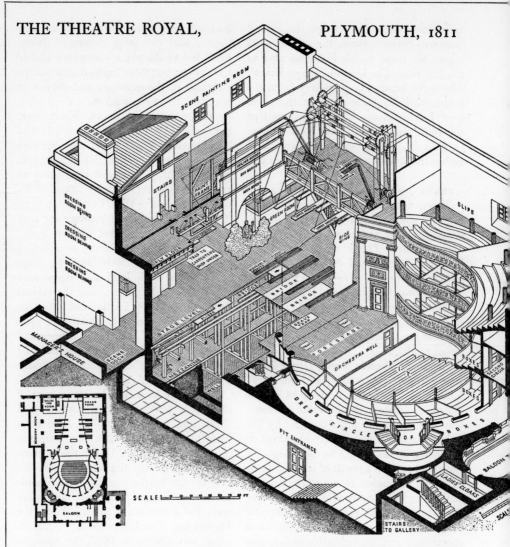

Above the stage are two galleries, one on either side, called the 'fly floors', from these floors the borders and any flying scenery were worked; above these galleries is the ceiling of the stage on which are many pulleys supporting sets of lines, usually three lines to each border. There are four sets of wings and borders on this stage, consisting in each case of three wings on each side and three borders. Only the rear set of borders can be seen in this drawing, consisting of an arch border, a sky border and a ceiling border. Each set of lines from all the arch borders is connected to a long wooden roller standing on the fly floor, and when a rope is pulled here the roller turns and all the arch borders move together; in the same way the other sets of borders can also be moved simultaneously. Attached to the underside of the fly floors are the upper-grooves which support the tops of the side wings. These are matched by bottom-grooves laid on the stage. In each group

A cut-open drawing of the theatre based on John Foulston's original designs.

you can see a short set of grooves for the side wings and a longer set for the halved flats to slide in. The longer top-grooves are hinged at the centre so that the ends can be lifted out of the way when not required; these too are joined to a roller.

At fly floor level is a room at the back of the stage used by the scene-painter, with a large wooden paint-frame on which scenery could be mounted and lowered through a slot in the floor to enable the artist to reach the whole area to be painted.

The stage, which raked up from front to back, was not a simple floor, but was designed with many openings. Here three sections of stage are named as 'bridges'. In the rear bridge position the centre portion of the stage, to the width of the proscenium opening, has divided into two parts which are being drawn off along sloping rails to fit underneath the side areas of the stage. When these sections had been drawn off by a man turning a windlass under the stage, there was a large hole in the floor.

In the drawing there are two floors below the stage, a mezzanine floor and a well. Each bridge normally stood at mezzanine level, as it was such a large platform it was very deep, so the well was provided for the lower part of the bridge to sink into. When a group of actors or actresses had arranged themselves on the bridge at mezzanine level, and the stage had opened above, the stage hands began to turn the windlass and the bridge was raised to stage level. There were smaller, but similar, units known as 'traps'. The two smaller traps on the fore-stage each allowed one man to be raised or shot up through the stage, the sudden appearance of a demon king being contrived in this way. These traps were not easy things to use and there are records of people being injured, or even killed, when using them. There were several different types of trap, one being the 'grave trap', which would have been used for 'Hamlet'.

elegant style. By a curtailment of the use-less portion of the stage in front of the curtain, and advancing the Orchestra and Lights near the Actors and Scenic Effects, the Lessee has been enabled to appro-priate the portion so obtained to form a certain number of Orchestra Stalls, which can be retained for the parties taking them for the whole of the Evening."

So, having first pushed the actor back into the picture, the management made a virtue of the need to move the lights closer to his now remote position and appropriated the 'useless' area of stage. This movement on the part of the man-agement did provide more seats, but it did not take account of the fact that most theatres were designed to allow the audience to see the actors on the fore-stage; with the actor behind the proscen-ium opening, the audience in the side seats were no longer well placed to see him. When the Haymarket was rebuilt in 1880 a gilt 'picture-frame' completely encircled the stage opening, and there was no sign at all of any fore-stage.

In spite of the restrictions concerning the presentation of drama at any place but the two Patent Theatres, there had been a gradual growth of theatres in London and elsewhere. In some cases, as at Bath, Royal Patents had been given to the theatres, whilst those at the royal places of residence, such as Brighton and Windsor, were licensed by the Lord Chamberlain. In 1788, however, an Act was passed which gave local Justices the power to grant licences to players for a period of sixty days at any one time. In 1843 the monopoly of the Patent Theatres was finally ended by an Act for Regulat-ing the Theatres, which allowed any

theatre to present 'legitimate' drama. The use of the term legitimate stems from the difference between the drama proper pre-sented at the Patent Theatres and those mixed-up versions of plays and musical entertainments which the non-patent theatres had to indulge in.

HISTORICAL ACCURACY

Although the order of the day in the larger theatres was for spectacle, interest in historical accuracy—such as is shown in the novels of Sir Walter Scott—aroused a demand for correct detailing in theatri-cal productions, particularly with regard to the scenes and costumes. William Capon—who redecorated the second Theatre Royal, Drury Lane, not long before it was pulled down—designed a complete new set of scenery for the new theatre. Both Capon and Kemble, the actor-manager, had an interest in histori-cal accuracy and their productions of Shakespeare's plays were set in correct pictorial representations of actual places. For 'King Richard III' Capon painted "The Tower of London, restored to its earlier state", and for another play "The ancient palace of Westminster, as it was about three hundred years back; from partial remains and authentic sources of information—put together with the great-est diligence and accuracy."

It was not only in the scenery that accuracy was to be found but also in the costumes. Until this time it was still general for the actors to be costumed in the fashions of their own time, except in the case of oriental, classical or similar figures. Garrick's witches in 'Macbeth' had been dressed in mittens, plaited caps, laced aprons, red stomachers and ruffs,

Mr PALMER as AHASUERUS in the TRIUMPH of the JEWISH QUEEN
London,Published by J.REDINGTON,73,Hoxton Street,Formerly called 208,Hoxton Old Town.

as Richard III drew crowds wherever the play was performed. Although audiences had in the past been drawn to the theatres to see individual players, we now find that the managements were deliberately building up a 'star' system, creating productions which were built around the star performer, but in spite of all their efforts neither the Theatre Royal nor Covent Garden was having an easy time. In 1846 the latter theatre was reconstructed and reopened as the Royal Italian Opera House, only to be destroyed by fire in 1856, on the occasion of a masked ball: the present theatre was opened in 1858.

Many theatres were now springing up in London and the country; among others was Sadler's Wells, which gave spectacular water and equestrian shows. It was here in 1782 that Joseph Grimaldi made

but in Kemble's production they were dressed not as ordinary people but as supernatural beings.

In the preceding century Shakespeare's plays had been altered and adapted to enable them to be performed at the non-patent theatres, but now, although Kemble and others returned to the earlier versions, they nevertheless cut and edited the plays to suit the new scenic requirements.

Acting as well as costumes and scenery was undergoing a change. Garrick had introduced characterisation into his performances in place of the grandiloquent rhetoric that had preceded him. When Edmund Kean followed Kemble at Drury Lane he brought a realism to his playing of villains that struck terror even among his fellow actors; his performances

Mr ANDERSON as MACBETH.
London,Published by J.REDINGTON,73,Hoxton Street,Formerly called 208,Hoxton Old Town.

53

his first appearance, when only three or four years old, in the role of a monkey, but he started his famous career as a clown in 'Robinson Crusoe', at Drury Lane. Another theatre well known today was the Royal Coburg, which opened in 1818, was renamed the Royal Victoria in 1833, and today is world famous as The Old Vic.

At this last theatre, and others like it, the public devoured the new plays which had begun to deal with social conditions, industrial unrest and the horrors of drink: 'The Factory Strike; or Want, Crime and Retribution', 'The Drunkard's Doom; or The Last Nail'. Virtue is triumphant in these plays, although the beautiful child may have to die to redeem her sinning father. Horrible murders such as 'Maria Marten, or Murder in the Red

Mr N. T. HICKS AS CLAUDE DUVAL. 43.
London, Published by J. REDINGTON, 73, Hoxton Street, Formerly called 208, Hoxton Old Town.

Barn', might be found at some of the lesser theatres, but they were more likely to be found at one or other of the hundreds of unlicensed theatres which sprang up in London in the early part of the nineteenth century, popularly known as Penny Gaffs. A typical play bill at Smith's Grand Theatre advertised: 'The Red Nosed Monster; or The Tyrant of the Mountains', to be followed by 'The Blood-Stained Handkerchief; or The Murder in the Cottage'. Like the Elizabethans before them the youthful audience were sometimes regaled with a dancing bear or performing dogs.

Edmund Kean's son Charles was to rise to fame in his management of the Princess's Theatre, where he continued the trend in realistic spectacular productions of Shakespeare and contemporary plays. These latter were mainly of a melodramatic and sentimental character by such authors as Dion Boucicault, who wrote 'The Long Strike' and 'Colleen Bawn', the latter play being famous for its lake scene contrived by the use of transparent gauzes. Gauzes played a large part in the plays of this period especially in dream sequences; a villain was usually unmasked by the revelation of his vile deeds in a prophetic dream. These effects were obtained by painting on the gauze with dyes, so that, when lit from the front, the gauze resembled the remainder of the painted scene, but when lit from behind a further scene or sometimes a tableau, would be revealed behind the gauze.

One difficulty which was always apparent in the use of painted scenes was the introduction of the distant view. In the early days the perspective scene was merely a backing to the actor performing

on the main stage, but now the actor performed amidst the scenery. To give the impression of distance the back scenes had to be built and painted to a smaller scale than they would have been in real life, so the actors had to keep away from these areas or they would have looked like giants. All sorts of dodges were used to get over this difficulty. In his book 'Blood and Thunder', Wilson Disher tells us that Kean, in his production of 'Pizarro', swung himself across a deep chasm on the branch of a tree and, after disappearing behind a rock, was replaced by a small dummy which moved among the back-scenes, thus fitting in with the distant scenery; an illusion which is said to have been most realistic in its effect.

If you wish to get a really good idea of the sort of scenery, plays and costumes in use at this time, you cannot do better than look at, or even buy, the sheets of settings and characters for the Juvenile Drama, which were, and still are, sold for children to cut out and use on their model theatres. Many of these scenes and costumes were based on the original London productions. They could originally be bought '1d plain, 2d coloured'. Today you can still buy many of them from the firm which carries on the famous name of Benjamin Pollock: 'The Miller and his Men' is one of his plays. The plot is typical of the period; it is set in the Forests of Bohemia, and deals with the Love of Claudine for the poor Hero, Lothair, and her troubles with the Villain, Grindoff the Miller, who is also the Leader of a Robber band. In all the plays written at this time the characters tended to be typed: beautiful heroines, handsome heroes and lovers—poor but honest, wicked villains and pathetic old men.

THE CHANGING SCENE

The new interest in social plays is probably best illustrated by the plays of Thomas Robertson; writing in the 1860's his best known play is 'Caste'. Robertson tried to break away from the stock characters and unreal situations of the melodramas and present instead problems of real life. This in turn affected the settings, which were now required to portray more accurately the actual homes of the characters. There was too a general dissatisfaction with the wing and border setting;

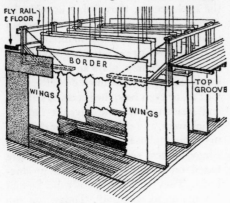

Wing and border setting

and complaints became frequent concerning their limitations. Actors were criticised for making their entries between the wings in positions where no door was painted; patrons objected to seeing the stage carpenters, in their paper hats, leading on the flats so that they should not jam in the grooves, and leaving dirty marks where they grasped the edges of the scenery. The occupants of the stage boxes objected to being able to see beyond the boundaries of the scene into the wings of the stage, where actors and stage hands could be seen awaiting their cue or enjoying a drink. Objections were also raised to the joints which could always be seen where each pair of flats met. Certainly if one was looking for realism the wing and flat system was not the answer and other ideas were sought.

One idea was to return to the earlier arrangement of wings set at an angle to the footlights, which was certainly better for masking in the sides of the scene; finally they were set to form one continuous wall giving the impression of a proper room. These walls had practical doors, which could be opened and closed although, of course, they were made of timber and canvas. The first use of such a 'box' set is credited to Madame Vestris, who introduced the idea from France between 1832 and 1841, whilst she was managing the Olympic Theatre in London. This was not, however, the true box set which we know today, as the ceiling was still represented by borders so that the overhead gas lighting battens could be used.

A member of the audience for Kean's spectacular productions had been Duke George II of Saxe-Meiningen, and on

Backstage at a Victorian Theatre

returning to his own country he set about building up a resident theatrical company, which differed from the current 'star productions' in that every member of the company was considered of equal importance. Like Kean, the Duke was concerned with achieving historical accuracy, and he designed both sets and properties himself. All his drawings for settings included groups of actors, for he believed the movement of individuals and groups on the stage to be an integral part of the play. The settings made use of platforms and steps to allow the groups of players to be massed on different levels. The crowd scenes were most carefully rehearsed, the actors being grouped in small units each with its own movements and sounds. The Duke achieved the suggestion of great crowds and armies by allowing only a small part to be visible to the audience; in lighting too the Duke was an innovator, making use not only of gas, but contrasting it at times with the new electric lamps. His company toured all the main cities of Europe, and wherever it went it was greeted with great applause and enthusiasm. In 1881 the company came to England and played at Drury Lane, but although enthusiastically received, their immediate effect on the English theatre was not lasting, as the star system of actor-managers was by now too firmly planted.

Probably the best known of the actor-managers were Henry Irving who, with Ellen Terry as his leading lady, was established for many years at the Lyceum Theatre, and Beerbohm Tree who managed Her Majesty's Theatre. Irving was the first of the actor-managers to be knighted, and this social recognition went a long way in raising the status of actors from that of rogues and vagabonds. Probably Irving's best known play was 'The Bells', but he staged many sumptuous productions of Shakespeare, among which was a production of 'Henry VIII', with music by Edward German, outstanding in its lavishness.

The end of the 19th century was the period of the great scenic artists who carried on the traditions set earlier by de Loutherbourg. In contrast to Saxe-Meiningen's practice of designing all his scenes and costumes himself, the scenes for 'Henry VIII' were designed and painted by the scenic artists: William Telbin, Joseph Harker and Hawes Craven. In some instances Irving commissioned a well-known artist, but whilst the production of 'Coriolanus' was entirely designed by Sir Laurence Alma-Tadema, the scenery was painted by Harker and Craven.

In a description written in 1901 we can read "Within the last few years, however, great changes have taken place in theatre scenes, and it has become the custom not only to limit the number of scenes, but to build them up in a more or less solid manner on the stage, trusting to the intervals between the acts to replace one by another. In the play of 'Herod', brought out by Mr. Beerbohm Tree at Her Majesty's Theatre last year, there was only one scene. Variety of effect was obtained there, however, by a dexterous employment of the electric light, so that one came away with an impression, at all events, that considerable changes had been made during the course of the play. In the production, however, of any of Shakespeare's plays, and more especially of 'Coriolanus', not only is it impossible to curtail the number of scenes, but they must be of such a nature as to allow for their rapid shifting. . . . Accustomed as we have become of late to the solid nature of modern scenes and critical, therefore, as to the illusion produced by them in comparison with the drop scenes and side wings of old times, it is remarkable that Sir Laurence should have been able, with the latter only, to convey an impression of solidity in his representations which holds its own even when matched with the single spectacle in 'Herod' ".

Not everyone was happy about these spectacular productions of Shakespeare; not only had the plays to be adapted to suit the scenic requirements, but, as is suggested above, there were often waits and pauses occasioned by the scene changes.

In 1879 William Poel, dissatisfied with the commercialism of the theatre, started his movement towards a simplification of Shakespearian production. In the first

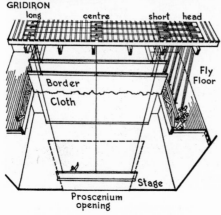

GRIDIRON

The hand-operated flying system

place he turned away from the acting editions of the plays then in use, back to the 'original' versions. In 1881 Poel staged 'Hamlet' on a bare draped platform, with no scenery and no intervals. In 1893 he built a replica of the Fortune Theatre on the stage of the Royalty Theatre, following this in 1895 by performances before the screens in the Hall of Gray's Inn, and later by a presentation of 'Twelfth Night' in the Hall of the Middle Temple, where, tradition says, it was first performed before Queen Elizabeth I; in this instance he built a stage based on de Witt's drawing. He next turned his attention to the Morality plays, and produced 'Everyman' in the Master's Court at Charterhouse. These productions were eventually to have their effect, but the picture stage was too well founded for them to have much immediate effect on the general run of presentations.

In the quotation above mention was made of 'drop scenes'. These were made possible by an adaptation of theatre design; until now the arrangement seen at Plymouth (page 50) was standard, only the canvas borders, the roller cloths, and perhaps some special items, being hung from the stage ceiling. But, as the height of auditoriums increased with additional tiers of circles and galleries, so the ceilings over the stages could be correspondingly higher. Previously the use of cloths had required that they be hung on rollers, but the constant rolling and unrolling was harmful to the painting; with greater height it became possible to raise a cloth —drop scene—vertically out of sight. The ceiling over the stage was now an open timber floor known as the 'grid', on this numerous pulleys were mounted to

Her Majesty's Theatre, 1897

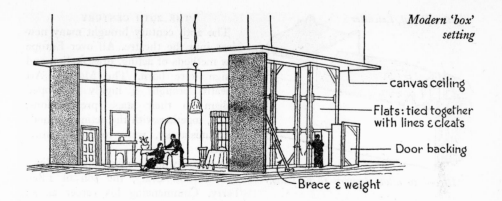

canvas ceiling

Flats: tied together with lines & cleats

Door backing

Brace & weight

enable cloths or borders to be hung in any position parallel with the front of the stage. These sets of pulleys were spaced at close intervals from front to back of the stage: each set comprised four pulleys, one over the centre of the stage and two more spaced equally from this within the width of the proscenium opening; over each a rope descended to the cloth or border, its opposite end being carried over a head-block directly above the edge of the fly floor; from there it descended to be tied off around a cleat fastened to the fly rail. When scenery was to be raised the three ropes were untied from their cleat, pulled until the scenery had reached the required height, and once again tied off.

By 1888 the architect J. G. Buckle was to say, "It should be possible in a well constructed stage to draw up the 'Cloths' without rolling or folding", and that "The height of the stage—i.e. from the floor to the underside of the 'Gridiron'—should be twice that of the proscenium opening". Referring to the scene grooves he said, "These survivals of antiquated methods are entirely dispensed with in the

more recent theatres, when the scenery is strapped together by cleats and cords, and secured to the floor of the stage by means of rods or braces, hooked to eyes attached to the framework of the scenery, whilst the other end is secured to the floor with 'stage screws'". This method is still used today, although extending wood braces generally replace the iron rods.

The flying of scenery was to affect theatres all over the country. When the Theatre Royal, Leicester, was built in 1836 there was one roof over the whole building, the space within it, over both auditorium and stage, being used by the scene painter; but in 1889 the Directors' Annual Report announced that "The roof and walls (of the stage) have been

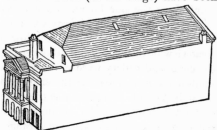

Theatre Royal, Leicester, as originally built

Theatre Royal, Leicester

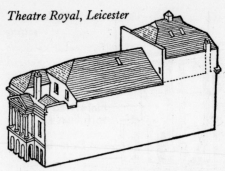

Altered to allow scenery to be flown

raised an additional sixteen feet in height, which enables the scenes to 'hang' without being rolled up or folded, which not only prevents damage to the scenes by creasing, but also allows twice the number of scenes to be used."

As the new 'realistic' plays required their settings to resemble real rooms, the scenic walls had to be arranged at varying angles and positions, and it was soon found that the old grooves, bridges and sloats could no longer be used and they became obsolete, only the traps remaining usable.

Buckle also dealt with the auditorium, and stressed the importance of each member of the audience being able to hear and see well; he was particularly vehement about the side boxes. When Beerbohm Tree rebuilt Her Majesty's in 1897 the auditorium was designed to allow a clear view of the stage from all the seats; the circle and gallery were arranged on a shallow arc directly facing the stage and the only possible exception was the stage boxes which, flanked by columns, still reflected the earlier proscenium arrangement.

The 20th century brought many new ideas into the theatre. All over Europe new methods of acting, presentation and design were born. The Moscow Art Theatre brought a highly developed realism to their stage presentations, which, together with the acting methods of Stanislavsky, were to have lasting effects.

One man who thought along new lines was Gordon Craig, the son of Ellen Terry. Commencing his career as an actor at the Lyceum, he rapidly became dissatisfied with the commercial theatre. In his early productions he replaced the naturalistic setting by simple curtains, screens, and effects of light: a single shaft of coloured light suggested the stained glass window of a church for 'Much Ado About Nothing'. He did away with the flat picture effect which resulted from the use of footlights and lights placed behind borders and wings, and used directional lighting made possible by new developments in electricity.

Craig, finding little support for his ideas in England, turned to Europe for his later productions, for which he designed settings relying for their effect on simplicity and good proportion; soon he was experimenting with the effects of changing light on simple architectural forms. In 1912 he prepared designs for a production of 'Hamlet' in Moscow, and in 1926 for Ibsen's 'The Crown Pretenders' at the Royal State Theatre, Copenhagen. In this production he made use of a great flight of steps, the effect of which could be varied from scene to scene by the use of screens, banners, costumes and the grouping of the actors; in addition Craig used here one of the new inventions of the period, the projection of scenic effects by light onto a plain sky-cloth hung around the stage.

He called for a new idea of theatre in which the productions would be under the control of one master-mind, the designer-producer, but in spite of his desire to re-shape the spirit of the theatre, Craig's realised productions did not succeed in breaking away from the picture-frame stage. The same may be said of Adolph Appia who created equally fine settings, using three dimensional scenery together with the symbolic use of light. Appia placed the actor first and foremost, and believed that the audience should not be distracted by over-elaborate painted scenery. He disliked the contrast between the reality of the actor and the flatness of the scenery, and tried to surround the three-dimensional actor with three-dimensional scenery, achieving his effects of distance by the use of light on a sky-cloth rather than by painted perspective.

The naturalistic picture theatre, however, received constant fuel in the form of new mechanical devices designed to enable elaborately built-up scenes to be changed easily and quickly; hydraulic, and later electric, lifts could change the shape of a stage in a moment, and sliding stages quickly replaced one built-scene by another. The adaptation of the old Japanese device of a revolving stage allowed many scenes to be built at the same time, any one of which could be revealed by a turn of the stage. Even the hand-operated flying system (page 59) was simplified by replacing the ropes by wires attached to counter-weights, thus balancing the weight of the scenery and simplifying its movement.

In the scenery itself doors and windows and real mouldings replaced the painted canvas of former days. Real rooms needed real effects of daylight and this could be provided by new ways of using electric light; instead of representing the open sky by a back-cloth and canvas borders, looking as one critic put it "like dirty washing hanging up to dry", the whole acting area was enclosed by a great canvas, or plaster, dome known as a cyclorama or sky-cloth. Solid pieces of scenery could be placed in front of this, and the problems of masking in the sides of the stage were solved by its use. This invention was first used in Germany by Mariano Fortuny who achieved an even effect of sunlight by projecting white light onto bands of coloured silk acting as reflectors to diffuse the light over the whole scene. Did we say the cyclorama was a new invention? Perhaps we should remember that a similar idea was used at the Teatro Olimpico.

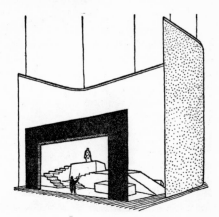

Cyclorama setting

One of Craig's main dreams, the control of a production by one man, is something that has in part become a feature of present-day theatre; one of the earliest 'producers' was Max Reinhardt who, using a permanent company, but no star system, staged his early plays with great realism. It is not, however, so much for his picture-frame productions or for his use of the revolving stage that we look to Reinhardt, but to his later productions for which he first used an old circus building, and later a new theatre built on similar lines, the Grosses Schauspielhaus in Berlin. In the first he staged 'Oedipus Rex' for which he used large crowds after the Meiningen manner, in the latter he staged 'Danton'; here the stage projected right forward into a horse-shoe auditorium so that Danton made his defence direct to the audience who surrounded him and merged with the actors to form the Revolutionary Assembly. One of his most famous productions was 'The Miracle', which he staged in England at Olympia, transforming the building into a cathedral, thus achieving unification of actor and audience. This movement to greater communion between the actor and audience was also to be found in his open-air presentation of 'Everyman' before the west front of Salzburg Cathedral.

Other experiments to break away from the picture-frame stage consisted in a return to a permanent architectural stage: such theatres were built in Düsseldorf and in Munich; these were supposed to be reconstructions of Shakespearean stages, but were more like a Roman stage with its centre door enlarged to form a

Reinhardt's 'Danton' in the Grosses Schauspielhaus

64

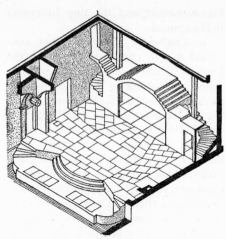

Permanent setting at the Vieux Colombier, Paris

small picture-frame stage. The most experimental of the various permanent theatres was the Vieux Colombier in Paris, built by Jacques Copeau and Louis Jouvet. The architectural setting here was solidly built in concrete, but its lack of points of entry was very limiting on the productions, and before long the audience tired of seeing much the same setting for every play; although attempts to alter its appearance were made they only tended to emphasise the continuity of the setting.

The visit of the Russian Ballet to Paris in 1909 introduced a new appreciation of the 'painted scene'; in this the painted scene did not pretend to be anything else but painting; bold, brilliant areas of colour made both scenes and costumes vibrant with life. One English designer affected by these productions was Claude Lovat Fraser, who designed a simple permanent setting for a revival in 1920 of 'The Beggar's Opera'.

One major influence at work on the theatre was found in the revolutionary theatre in Russia. In the period directly following the first World War the Russian theatre was in a very experimental state, and settings were designed in many differing forms: cubistic, constructivist. The latter settings consisted simply of such scaffolding as was required to build up the necessary acting levels. There was no attempt in these productions to make real pictures, the audience were expected to contribute their imaginations to the player's efforts; even the lighting units were hung up in full view and, although most productions were performed on existing picture-frame stages, at least one producer, Eisenstein, mixed his theatre with something closely resembling circus performances.

One theatre which broke away from the picture-frame stage and influenced thought today was the Realistic Theatre of Okhlopkov; this was a rectangular room containing both actors and audience. There was no permanent stage, the acting area being rearranged for each individual play; at one time it might be placed against one wall with platforms projecting among the seats, at another it could be placed in the middle of the hall. For the production of 'Mother', Okhlopkov arranged a narrow platform around the walls of the hall behind the audience, with steps leading, by gangways, to a central circular platform; in this way the actors were placed in direct contact with their audience. On entering the lighted hall the audience saw the stage open before them; when the lights were lowered their attention was focused on a particular place by the use of directed

Production of 'Mother' at the Realistic Theatre, Moscow

light. Only such properties as were essential to the performance were used, but in its simple condition the drama could be even more real in that the audience were directly involved in the action of the play, and felt each character to be one of them, as indeed they were, both actors and audience being all revolutionaries together.

In England the commercial theatre remained much the same in the new century. The picture-frame still dominated the scene, although there were moves to simplify the scenery by using drapes or curtains, and one or two expressive pieces of scenery. Experiments in performing Shakespeare included fore-stages built out over the orchestra pit, whilst the historically correct costumes were replaced, sometimes even by modern dress. The really experimental work, however, was carried on in small theatres sponsored by enthusiasts, such as The Lyric,

Hammersmith, and the tiny Everyman in Hampstead.

At Cambridge, Terence Gray converted a 19th century theatre into the Festival Theatre, removing the picture-frame and extending the stage forward so that it ended in a flight of steps within the auditorium, the stage itself being surrounded by a plaster cyclorama which enclosed the settings. Gray looked upon his stage as a platform for the actors, and preferred his scenery to consist of simple platforms, ramps, steps, screens or three-dimensional shapes. These units were lit so that they fitted with the changing moods of the play, and little attempt was made to present realistic effects. The movement and grouping of actors on the platform were arranged for their dramatic effect, and a close relationship between actor and audience was underlined by making many of the entrances and exits through the auditorium. The recognition of the actors as persons dressed up was looked upon by Gray as of value in reminding the audience that they were at a play and not living reality. To this end in one production he copied the Russian method of showing the audience all the workings of the stage, with no concealment of stage hands, waiting actors or scenic equipment.

At the Old Vic in London, under the control of Lilian Baylis, the system of a permanent company performing a repertory of plays throughout a season was introduced, in contrast to the method used in the 'West End' theatres of assembling a company for a play which would run as long, or as short, a time as the public were prepared to support it. The repertory system was appreciated by the

66

actors as it relieved them, for a season, of financial care—although salaries were not large—and allowed them wider opportunities in the range of plays performed; these included revivals and modern plays, but more especially the plays of Shakespeare. Here many of the ideas dreamed of by Poel were realised both in the staging and speaking of the plays. In the season 1939–40, Tyrone Guthrie varied the system so that plays performed during the season were given on different nights instead of being performed for a week or so and then replaced by another play.

Shakespeare's plays were also performed at the Shakespeare Memorial Theatre, Stratford-on-Avon, erected in 1877. This building was burnt down in 1926 and a competition held for a new design was won by Miss Elizabeth Scott. The design, in the main, followed the picture-frame tradition, with a stage provided with mechanical contrivances to facilitate the changing of scenery. In front of the proscenium opening was a fore-stage capable of variation or complete removal, flanked on either side by two bastions whose tops formed open galleries or balconies, and with doors at stage level. The auditorium was fan-shaped, with circles or galleries directly facing the stage. At the time of building, the tendency in interior decoration was to do away with the gilt and cupids of the Victorian theatre, and as a result the side walls of the auditorium, bereft of boxes, displayed large areas of bare plaster. This had the unfortunate effect of creating a feeling of great distance between the circles and the stage, an impression which has since been partly overcome by the introduction of open boxes built out from the side walls. The proscenium area has also been adapted in an attempt to break down the feeling of remoteness which was experienced by many actors on this stage.

REPERTORY, LITTLE THEATRES AND THE OPEN STAGE

In place of the old circuits a system of repertory theatres grew up in many of the larger cities. One of the earliest of these was Miss Horniman's Gaiety Theatre, opened in Manchester in 1907. This was closely followed, in 1911, by the Liverpool Playhouse which is still running, as is also the Birmingham Repertory Theatre built in 1912, and opened by Sir Barry Jackson the following year. In the 1920's repertory companies sprang up in many centres, and typical of these is the Northampton Repertory Players, who in 1927 reopened the late 19th century Opera House and Theatre Royal; they, unlike many of their predecessors, have remained open ever since.

Whilst the majority of these repertory companies performed in existing theatres or in converted halls, some players toured the country performing wherever they found suitable premises; such were The Pilgrim Players, who performed morality and modern verse plays with little or no scenery in churches and church halls.

The tremendous upsurge of theatrical interest throughout America has led there to the building of many theatres, particularly in the universities where a theatre is considered essential, and many companies who cannot afford a 'proper' theatre have realised that a proscenium opening and stage machinery are not always necessary to the performance of a

Open-stage production of 'The Three Estates' in the Assembly Hall, Edinburgh

play. They have taken their cue from the productions of the Realistic Theatre of Russia, and use existing halls with the audience arranged around a part of the floor which forms the stage. Here, amid their audience the actors perform on their 'arena' stages, using a minimum of furniture and scenery.

In Great Britain similar experiments have been made. Theatre in the Round has been seen in Scarborough and London, and at the Edinburgh Festival of 1948 Tyrone Guthrie introduced an 'open' stage into the Assembly Hall. Here he produced 'The Three Estates' by Sir David Lyndsay. The stage projected into the hall and was surrounded on three sides by the audience seated in the body of the hall and in the galleries, the fourth side

having a scenic backing with entries for the actors. A similar arrangement is used in the Arena theatre, Birmingham.

In this trend towards open-stage theatres Bernard Miles built his first Mermaid Theatre, which was a small private theatre designed in the Shakespearian manner, followed by his second Mermaid in the City of London.

Much experimental work in the 1920's was carried out by groups of amateurs who built their own theatres, and the same trend can be seen today at Middlesbrough, and in the new theatre which the Questors are building at Ealing. In this one building it will be possible to have a whole variety of stage arrangements, enabling plays to be performed in many of the ways which we have seen in use at one time or another in the long journey we have made from primitive times. Here we have a new theatre which attempts to break free from the limitations that had settled so solidly on theatre building through the last century, and we can only hope that it will meet with the success that it deserves.

CONCLUSION

If you have read this far you will have realised that the theatre is capable of being expressed in many and various ways. Indeed there are many other forms which we have been unable to mention, but all have something theatrical about them: the circus, the music hall, opera, ballet, and even the cinema and television. All these have their own forms and ways of expressing themselves; perhaps we can take something from each to add new life to the others.

Today many theatres are dying and closing in the British Isles; maybe this is because many are still trying to present a remote picture to their audience seated apart from the actor in a darkened and, in many cases, none too comfortable audi-torium. Today this same sort of picture can be brought into our own homes and we do not need to leave the comfort of our armchairs or warm fires to see it.

It looks as though a new sort of theatre may be needed, or perhaps not so new—most forms have been tried somewhere before—but a form which allows us to take a part with the actors in the creation of the play, and allows us the opportunity and enjoyment of mixing with other people.

When you wish then to take part in a play do not be put off because you may not have all the paraphernalia of a picture stage. Remember that 'a board, two trestles and a deal of passion', can also make a play, and do not jump too quickly to the conclusion that any one form of theatre is right or wrong—the proper form depends on the particular problem of the moment.

If this book were an arena stage we should now have to turn to you and say "The Play is finished, the book is done, you can put it down", but, as we still, for the present, have a picture-frame stage, we can show this is the end by "Ringing Down the Curtain".

The Questors Theatre, Ealing.
An open-stage production

69

A Select Book List

By Elizabeth N. Bewick

(See also the book list to "Shakespeare and his plays")

ALLEN, JOHN. *Going to the theatre.* ("Excursions" series.) Phoenix, 1949. Illus. Booklist. How a play is rehearsed, produced, dressed, staged and acted; with some information on the management of a theatre.

BRITISH DRAMA LEAGUE. *The Player's library: the catalogue of the library of the British Drama League.* Faber, 1950. Three supplements, 1951, 4, 6. Alphabetically arranged under author, giving details of type of play, number of acts and scenes, scenery, costume and incidental music.

BROOK, DONALD. *A pageant of English actors.* Rockliff, 1950. Illus. Booklist. Brief biographies of famous actors representing all periods of English drama from the time of Shakespeare to the present day.

The romance of the English theatre. Rockliff. Rev. edn., 1952. Illus. A history of the English theatre for the general reader.

BRIDGES-ADAMS. *The irresistible theatre. Vol. 1. From the Conquest to the Commonwealth.* Secker & Warburg, 1957. Illus. Booklist. A detailed survey setting the history of the theatre against the social background of the period, with an appendix listing the Medieval Mysteries.

BURTON, H. M. *Shakespeare and his plays.* ("Outlines.") Methuen, 1958. Illus. Booklist. An outline study of Shakespeare the man and the dramatist, and an evaluation of his works and their importance in literary history.

CHAMBERS, SIR E. K. *The Medieval stage.* 2 vols. O.U.P. 1903. A comprehensive and authoritative account for the serious student, covering minstrelsy, folk drama, and religious drama.

The Elizabethan stage. 4 vols. O.U.P. 1923. The standard history of the period for the serious student, covering the Court; the Companies and playhouses; staging; plays, playwrights and anonymous works.

CLEAVER, JAMES. *The theatre through the ages.* Harrap. Repr. 1948. Illus. Booklist. A short guide to the history of the theatre and the social conditions in which it has flourished, from the days of ancient Greece to the present time, with a select list of plays.

DENT, EDWARD J. *A theatre for everybody: the story of the Old Vic and Sadlers Wells.* Boardman. 1946. Illus. Booklist. A history of two famous theatres with some account of the plays and operas performed there over the years.

ELLIS, RUTH. *The Shakespeare Memorial Theatre.* Winchester. 1948. Illus. Booklist. A popular history of the theatre and its place in the history of Shakespeare's town, with an appendix listing the "birthday" plays from 1879 to 1948.

HARTNOLL, PHYLLIS, ED. *The Oxford companion to the theatre*. O.U.P. 2nd edn. 1957. Booklist. An alphabetical dictionary of theatrical information covering the theatre in all ages and all countries, with a supplement of illustrations chronologically arranged and indexed.

HODGES, C. WALTER. *Shakespeare and the players*. Benn. 1948. A book for children.

HODGES, C. WALTER. *The Globe restored*. Benn. 1953.

KEMP, T. C., and TREWIN, J. C. *The Stratford festival: a history of the Shakespeare Memorial Theatre*. Cornish. 1953. Illus. The history of the Shakespeare festival giving details of actual productions, a list of plays performed from 1879–1953 and the players in successive festival companies.

LAVER, JAMES. *Drama, its costume and decor*. Studio. 1951. Illus. Booklist. A detailed history of stage designing, decor and costume from the time of the ancient Greeks to the present day.

MANDER, RAYMOND, and MITCHENSON, JOE. *A picture history of the British theatre*. Hulton. 1957. Illus. A pictorial record of the achievements of the British theatre from 1576 to 1957, chronologically arranged.

NICOLL, ALLARDYCE. *British drama: an historical survey from the beginnings to the present time*. Harrap. 4th edn. 1949. Booklist. The standard general history for the serious student.

The development of the theatre: a study of theatrical art from the beginnings to the present day. Harrap. 4th edn. 1958. Illus. Booklist. An outline history of the art of the theatre with special reference to the English stage.

A history of English drama, 1660–1900. 4 vols. C.U.P. Rev. edns. 1952–5. Successive volumes cover Restoration drama, early eighteenth century drama, late eighteenth century drama and early nineteenth century drama in great detail, with handlists of plays and dates of first performances. (Vol. 5. Late nineteenth century drama, in preparation.)

Masks, mimes and miracles: studies in the popular theatre. Harrap, 1931. A specialised study for the serious student.

World drama from Aeschylus to Anouilh. Harrap. Repr. 1951. Illus. A general view of world drama from ancient Greece to modern times.

SOUTHERN, RICHARD. *Changeable scenery: its origin and development in the British theatre*. Faber. 1952. Illus. Diagrams. A specialised study for the interested reader.

THOMPSON, LAURENCE. *Behind the curtain: an introduction to the theatre*. Ward Lock. 1951. Illus. The story of the Old Vic training school and the Young Vic theatre.

WALTON, CECILE. *The children's theatre book for young dancers and actors*. Black. 1949. Illus. An introduction to stage costume and make-up.

Index

Date Due